The Stranger
in My House

The Stranger in My House

How to Reconnect to Your Child with Mental Illness

By Corrie Corrigan

UN-SETTLING BOOKS
Boulder, Colorado USA

Cover Design & Typography: Sally Wright Day
Cover Photography: Tatyana Gladskih
Editing: Maggie McReynolds
Author's photo courtesy of Jordan Lindo

This book is dedicated to my family with love:
My children, Zachary and Codi,
My parents, Catherine, John Bill, and John Corrigan,
And my siblings, John, Jessica, and David Corrigan.

I couldn't imagine getting through
all of this without any of you!
I am and will always be
eternally grateful for all of you.

judgments, the self-shame, and the isolation with such rawness that if you are a parent with a child who struggles, you will relate to this book. Corrie gives you practical tools that, the more you practice them, become your daily habits, leading you to healthier home. Her message is one of compassion, and love—not just a mother's love, but self-love as well. Corrie tells it like it is, doesn't try to sugar coat the ugliness of mental health, and doesn't rub your back and tell you that life is all going to fine. Instead, she gives it to you straight—and straight from her heart. This book, the vulnerability within it, and the strength of her words will change your life. If you have been searching for that one thing that can shift your life, and the life of your child, this is it.

—Laura Thomas
Mental Health Advocate and Mindset Coach

Contents

Foreword

There are no words for how impactful this book is. How important it is that we all raise our voices and share our experiences with mental illness. That there is nothing shameful about having a child with mental illness, and, in truth, once you have implemented the incredible strategies Corrie offers in this book, you will see the incredible gifts that living through all this has provided for you.

I've been blessed to witness the transformation that transpired as Corrie tested and tried every strategy and piece of advice she offers in this book, and it has been life-changing to watch.

Corrie is one of the most passionate people I know, and when she puts her mind to doing something, she does it. So when it came time to take her power back and rebuild her relationship with her son, she did it with so much love and conviction that I was inspired.

Reading this book is like finding the light after being lost in the dark for so long you have forgotten what the light looked like.

Corrie's bravery in telling her story to break the stigma around mental illness, and to offer support for others going through the same thing, is what is going to make a real difference in the mental health system. No one understands what it is like to live this life except someone who has lived through it.

This book is refreshing in its honesty and truth. There is nothing clinical in these pages. This book is filled with everything you need to heal the relationship between you and your child. This book is a gift. I wish it had been written when I felt I had nowhere to turn.

—Tamara Arnold

Author of *The Magical Business Method*
St. Catharines, Ontario

Introduction

It all started for me the day I got a phone call at work from a family friend, telling me my son Codi had seriously cut himself and was bleeding profusely. He'd cut himself before, but the result had been shallow wounds intended not to end his life but to mask the internal pain he felt. This time, however, was different. This was further than he'd ever gone, and he was terrified.

I panicked. Nothing else existed around me. It was exactly like you see in the movies: people were talking, but I couldn't make out what they were saying. Everything seemed to be happening in slow motion. My heart was racing, and my eyes filled with tears. Instantly, my whole world fell apart.

The voice on the other end of the phone suddenly came into clarity. He was telling me that he was with Codi and that he was going to deal with the situation and make sure Codi was okay. I asked for Codi to be brought to me. I needed to see my son, to see that he was going to be alright. I was feeling all sorts of things in this moment: fear, panic, anger, sadness, and then, abruptly, the need to be sick.

You see, less than 24 hours before, Codi had been released from the hospital where he'd been admitted for a 72-hour assessment called a Form 1 here in Canada. He'd been cleared because they'd decided he wasn't a danger to himself or anyone else.

Over the years, I'd kept telling myself that if I could just get a psychological assessment for Codi and could figure out exactly what was going on and what he needed, everything would be fine. The night when the police had taken Codi to the hospital and had him admitted on a Form 1, I was actually hopeful this would be exactly what I needed to help my son. But once he was released from the hospital, I felt flattened by disappointment. We'd gotten no answers, just a dismissal. Everything I'd set myself up to hope for was shattered.

Then, not even a day later, Codi had cut himself. I knew in my heart I couldn't take him back to the hospital. For what? To tell them they were wrong? He wasn't ready to come home yet? He had already figured out exactly what to say to get released. In that moment I felt that, if I sent him back, he would just get out and attempt suicide again—only the next time, I wouldn't be getting a call for help. The next time, I would be burying my son. In that moment, I had the realization that Codi and I were on our own. It was going to be the two of us, finding a way out of this together.

I'd felt this panic before. I'd even been in this situation before—the first time, horribly, by getting a suicidal text message from Codi. Then, as now, the thought of losing my son, of having to move on without one of my children, played over and over in my head. It felt like the worst possible thought in the whole world.

Even though this was hideously familiar, it also felt different, like this might be my last chance to save my son. Deep down inside, I knew that this time, I needed to pull back from everything else and focus on making sure that Codi knew he was loved and that his life was his to live any way he wanted. He needed to see that he could be happy and healthy and that all he had to do was believe it and choose it. I had to have the strength of my convictions because I knew Codi did not. At this point, he wasn't even sure he wanted to live.

And so this became my challenge over the course of the next year: making sure that my son could see that life was worth living, that his life was more significant than all the pain and suffering he felt, and that he was loved more than he could even imagine. The stakes were high. This was Codi's third suicide attempt, and I was deeply scared that next time, if there were a next time, I would be planning his funeral.

My son is mentally ill. At that time, he was 16 years old, and we didn't yet have a clear diagnosis. But I knew that I needed to help him understand that, whatever was wrong, he was stronger than his demons. I wanted him to see that I was willing to fight for him and that he was worth fighting for, no matter what I might have to sacrifice.

Up until this point, I'd spent a lot of time berating myself. I'd put in many long days and many sleepless nights worrying about where I'd gone wrong. What had I done? What had I not done? What had I done that I could have done some other way? I played different times of my son's life over and over and blamed myself for everything I could possibly think of. If I had done this or that differently, would my son be different? Would he be happy? Would he have tried to kill himself several times?

Shortly after the call that day, I took a leave of absence from work. I was determined to figure out how I could help Codi. Every time I came up with a new idea, I tried it in the hopes of changing the way my son thought about the value of his life. For small periods of time, each new thing seemed to work—but then we would always seem to end up back at the same point of tension and despair. I felt like I was failing my son.

And that's how it went over the next year of our lives. I tried things and I failed, over and over again. One day I made a decision, and I tried something different, something completely unlike anything I'd tried up until then. I look back now and realize that it was on that day that I stopped failing and started to succeed. That day made all the previous failed attempts worth it. That day became the beginning of a new way of life for both me and my son, and the beginning of a better relationship between us. That decision was the beginning of what I am going to share with you in this book, along with the tools that worked for me. And that became the foundation of the life and the relationship that Codi and I have today.

I didn't come to this alone, though I felt alone for a long time. During that long and difficult year, I was surrounded by my friends and family, but I always felt isolated. How could anyone understand what I was going through or what my life was like behind closed doors? But that day, when things started to turn around for me and my son, was the day I learned that there *was* someone out there, someone just like me who knew exactly what I was going through and exactly what I was feeling because she had gone through the exact same thing and found the way out. That someone became my coach, my mentor, and my light through the darkness. With her help, I was able to create a new life for Codi and me.

And that's when I realized how important it is for those of us whose children struggle with mental illness to share our journeys. I knew that if I could help just one person, to give one person hope or make one person realize that I share in their shame and pain, then my story was the story I needed to tell.

I want you to know without a shadow of doubt that you, like me, are not alone. That once I was where you are right now, caught up in fear. That you are strong enough and that you have everything you need to create a fresh beginning for you and your child, just as I did with Codi.

I stand before you as someone who made changes,

who saw what once seemed hopeless turn around. You can do this too.

Once I started down this road of discovery in the world of mental illness, I became so aware of how many others were out there struggling, just like me and you. Others who feel, as I did and as you do, that they are alone in a system that constantly lets them down, leaving them with nowhere to turn. I want to tell them what I want to tell you: that I have found a way out, a way that works for both my son and for me. I want to share, with you and with the rest of the world, the successful strategies I've tried, tested, and use to this day.

I understand that it might be hard at this point to believe that anything will really help. You've become discouraged by a flawed system that fails so many. You've lost hope when each new person you think might be able to help you and your child instead passes you along to someone else because they don't know what to do or insist that your child isn't "that bad." You take a day off or schedule an appointment for your child, and then a day of war breaks out in your home because your child refuses to attend the appointment. Each new person or department or referral explaining how they wish they could help you, but the waiting list is so long with people "who actually want help." I can't even count the amount of times I waited for a referral for months only to go on a waiting list for months and then be told that I needed "to see someone else."

I did find a doctor at McMaster Hospital who was

fantastic. That was helpful. That made me feel like someone was listening to both Codi and me. We went a couple times. Codi was opening up. We were trying different medications to see what was working or not. And then one day, Codi decided he wasn't going anymore. We fought, and I tried to reason with him and get him to take his medication and be at the appointments and tried to get him to see that maybe this was the answer. He refused time and time again. Eventually the doctor had to remove Codi from the list. How do you explain that your child changes their behaviour minute by minute? Making an appointment is great for the office, but not for your child. Your child needs somewhere you can go at the drop of a hat. When they decide right now is the time they want to talk, or want help, or need to open up, the last thing you need is an appointment six months away.

It would be beyond gratifying to change the system, or at least make mental health professionals recognize the gaps so many families fall through when a diagnosis is unknown or unclear, or when an older child refuses treatment altogether. I know through personal experience how much it helps to be able to see that you can actually have a happier, healthier relationship with your child, to have hope at a time when hope seems like a thing of the past.

That's why I'm sharing my experience, my pain, and my way out. That's why I knew I needed to write this book—for you and every parent who needs to read it.

In the following chapters, you will learn what I did,

use the exercises attached to each chapter, and work toward discovering your child again. The child you know is still in there somewhere, just waiting to be found and loved. Let's find them together.

This Isn't Normal, Is It?

You're likely just where I and most of my clients started: lying awake at night and wondering whether this is just a stage your child is going through or something more serious. It feels big to you, but nobody else seems to notice—or if they do, they don't seem to be concerned about it.

Your family seems to be dismissing it as "just a phase" or even implying that it's your fault because you're raising your child on your own. Your babysitter is noticing your child is different, so you've had lengthy discussions about whether something's up due to lack of sleep, more sugar than usual, or maybe your child's reaction to the weekend they just spent with their dad. Teachers send notes more often, the calls from the school are becoming more frequent, and now you're being asked to either come pick up your child or keep them home for the next day or two.

But no matter how many people notice the changes, no one seems all that alarmed about them except you. So you try to push the anxiety out of your mind and go on with life as usual. Still, there's this nagging feeling you can't seem to shake. No matter how hard you try to convince yourself that everything is okay and things will return to normal, you still find yourself lying awake, wondering and worrying about your child.

One of my clients Sarah reached out again and again to her son Jonathan's school. Jonathan was starting to act out and misbehave in class. He was disruptive, and the teacher was having a hard time focusing on the other students because of Jonathan's behaviour. Each day was different: he would be loud and angry one day and cracking jokes the next. Frequently, he acted out and talked out of turn. It was worrisome to Sarah, but it seemed like both Jonathan and his school were accepting this as some kind of new normal.

Sarah tried to ask for help, to figure out what was going on. At first, she reached out through regular channels, checking in with Jonathan's teacher every day to see how things were going. When the school dismissed her concerns, she felt anxious. But when the school probed into what might be wrong at home, Sarah felt attacked, and made excuses about things the family was going through to try to explain some of her son's behaviour.

Finally, the school implemented a sticker reward system. If Jonathan was "good," he would get a sticker at the end of the day. If he got at least three for the week, the teacher promised to do something special during class with him.

But Jonathan never got three stickers in one week. Instead, he was removed from class. If it was close to the end of the day, he'd be sent to the school's resource room by the office to complete his work on his own. If it was early or in the middle of the day, he'd be essentially kicked out altogether, and Sarah would be told she needed to come pick him up. These "solutions," the school explained, were necessary so that Jonathan didn't disrupt the rest of the class, because it wasn't fair to the other students who were there trying to learn.

No one seemed to notice or care how disruptive this was to Sarah and her son, though. Sarah was interrupting her day to come get her son several times a week. Jonathan wasn't getting the education he needed. Sarah told me that this made her feel like the school figured it was ok to "sacrifice" Jonathan's education, like Jonathan wasn't important. Sending him home was the easy solution. At no time did the school offer Sarah or Jonathan any alternatives.

Another one of my clients Jennfer asked for an Educational Assistant (EA) for her daughter Olivia and was denied because Olivia didn't quite fit the criteria. So Olivia was moved to a different class, which didn't help, and ended up doing most of her work from home because the teacher couldn't get her to sit still or concentrate long enough to complete an assignment in school. It took Olivia almost two hours every night to do her schoolwork on her own.

Jennifer continued to try to advocate for her daughter, and eventually the school gave in and assigned Olivia an EA. It didn't help. The EA spent most of her time chasing Olivia around the school and trying to get her to either stay in class or stay on task. By this point, it had become a game for Olivia. She was amused by distracting the class, running the halls, and either hiding things around the school or checking on things she'd hidden on previous days to see if anyone had found them yet.

Even with all that disruption and the concerning aspects of her behaviour, Olivia was still meeting the minimum requirements to pass each grade. The school kept moving her along, advancing her from one grade to the next every year. There was no other help offered to Olivia or Jennifer to help Olivia manage or change her behaviour.

Me, I just felt lost when I had to deal with the school. No matter what I said or how often I reached out, it felt like no one was really listening or understanding what I was saying. Like so many of my clients, I was simply brushed off. My son passed each year because he was extremely smart, but his angry outbursts and trips to the office were getting worse and more frequent. You know that sinking feeling you get every time your phone rings and you look down to see the school's phone number? That became all too familiar during that time for me.

Failed by the System

Does it feel like the school is letting you down? You're right: it is. So, it seems, are the doctors and counselors, though it might take you a while to figure that out because you can't even get in to see a specialist. The whole referral process takes so many months that you end up forgetting altogether that it's in the works. There is so much going on, and you have so many appointments in your calendar.

When you do finally get in to see someone, appointment after appointment, doctor after doctor, it's always the same: you're told that your child has to be willing to participate. Except they aren't. And why should they? They don't see value in themselves, nor do they have any faith in the system.

I get it. I felt I'd been let down, and I felt I'd failed—so I wasn't exactly shocked that my son felt the same way. But I wasn't ready to give up, and neither are you. Like me, you try and talk your child into believing the system will work, even though you have little hope that it will. At this point, the only reason you keep trying to find a solution, or find the person who has the solution, is because your child needs you to. Your heart and gut instinct are telling you that these behaviour issues aren't just a stage, that they are a big deal, and that you need to figure something out, and fast!

Knowing there is something definitely wrong is one of the worst feelings, especially when you feel like you can't fix it because you aren't even sure what *it* is. I remember having to call my boyfriend or my cousin to come over because Codi was freaking out, throwing stuff, and punching holes in the walls. I was afraid to be alone with Codi and didn't know how to deal with him or know what to do. All I knew was that I felt the need to protect myself by making sure his anger didn't come my way.

It's a horrible thing when you feel like you have to protect yourself from your own child. You hear them yelling and instantly wonder where you can hide. You take inventory of who else is in your house to make sure nobody is going to aggravate the situation or get hurt, but at the same time, you want to make sure that someone besides you is home in case things get out of hand.

There's a sickening drop in your stomach and a tightness in your throat, every morning when you wake up. You lie there silently, listening to see if you can hear them. You wonder if they are awake yet and what kind of mood they are in. If they aren't up yet, you start to tiptoe around the house so you don't wake them and start the day of destruction you already fear is inevitable. You know deep down that nothing about this is normal or healthy. For me I knew my other son didn't have these same behaviours and didn't cause these same feelings in me. I wasn't hiding in my room from my other son. And Zachary wasn't the target of Codi's anger or his outbursts. I seemed to be. Well, me and whatever walls or furniture got in his way. Your situation may be different. You might have to take into account the safety of your other child.

On Your Own

This is where the isolation begins to really take hold. You've already cancelled plans and changed your social behaviours—if not consciously, then because you subconsciously felt that it was easier to do so. Like me and many of my clients, you've begun to give in to the nagging need to isolate yourself from everyone and everything out there. You probably don't even realize how long this has been in the making.

Of course, you still make plans. But half the time you suspect you're going to have to cancel, and the other half you simply agree without any intention of going just because you don't want to explain why you can't. I avoided getting pinned down all the time. "We'll see," I'd say. I had a teenager who technically should have been able to be left alone and yet, that was just impossible for me at that time. People didn't get it, and I didn't want to talk about it.

You're feeling that too. People just don't seem to understand the fear, the worrying about what will happen next—or when it will go down. By now, you've up even trying to explain it to people. Now you just say yes to invitations, and then deal with it later through a text message that says something like, "Something came up, sorry, not going to make it, maybe next time," or you say no and make up "something else" you've committed to.

You start to avoid people so they can't ask you to make plans. You've gotten good at coming up with reasons why people can't come over, because there's no way you want to risk them seeing what happens behind closed doors if or when your child decides to freak out. I mean, what if they come over and then all of a sudden, it's game on for your child because there's someone new to misbehave in front of? What if something happens and they go and start telling everyone what it's like? They'll tell people how your child behaves, and then those people will start to judge and talk about you and your child. It's all avoidable—as long as you don't go out and don't let others in.

That might be a price you're willing to pay—for a while. But then you look around and realize that all that you have is you and your child. You've shut everyone out by sacrificing what you want for what you think is in the best interest of all involved. And you're starting to get lonely. Tackling this all on your own exhausts you down to your very soul.

Every day blurs into the next. Just getting out of bed in the morning has become a monumental task. What will happen when your child gets up? What if you wake him and then the day starts off on the wrong foot? You lie there in bed with everything that's already happened playing through your mind. Then, all of a sudden, you hear your child's footsteps, and your whole body cringes. You hold your breath and wait, anticipating what is about to happen. Are they in a good mood or bad mood? Is this day going to start with you being flipped out of your bed and your stuff smashed? You're about to find out, starting any second now, as you hear your child's steps getting closer to your bedroom.

This is an awful way to live and think, and though you're struggling to change it, you're losing yourself more and more as the days go by. You just can't seem to make it better for your child. Long gone are the days when you could kiss their boo boos and make them happy. Nowadays nothing you do seems to make them happy.

Then, of course, there's the struggle of going out in public with your child. Can you do it today or not? Quick trips, like to Tim Horton's for coffee or the store for milk, may go off fairly easily just by buying your child something while you're out. But a major grocery trip or going to a football game or something of that nature? Forget it! Going out for more than a quick stop inevitably brings on an "episode" of some sort. Walking though the mall, your child will cause a scene for sure and will start talking loudly or yelling and swearing. You'll start to walk faster, but it won't matter. The people around you will already be looking. They'll know that this unruly, out- of-control child is yours.

One Step Forward, Two Steps Back

You feel stuck between wanting to help your child and wanting to just throw in the towel. You wish you could somehow go back to how things were right before they got bad, but you know that's impossible. Those times seem like a movie or something you dreamt up. Nothing about your life resembles how or who you used to be. You are alone. You feel isolated. You feel hopeless. You feel like curling up in a fetal position and just crying for days or weeks at a time—actually, you've probably actually done that once or twice. Nobody in your life understands how you feel, which only creates a stronger sense of isolation and loneliness. Who are you now, and what is it going to take for you to show your child that there is a better life? A happier life—one that they can actually enjoy and be proud of? Right now, the way you feel seems uncomfortably like the way your child feels about life. The only difference is that you know somewhere in the depth of your heart or soul that it *can* get better, and your child doesn't believe that for one second.

You have no one to turn to because you are far too afraid of the judgment. You've already heard what others think. You know all too well that they feel that:

- You are "enabling" your child
- You need to keep him medicated
- You should make him go live with his dad

- You need to put him in foster care
- You should make him move out
- You are contributing to his behaviour

You can handle this. You don't like it, but you can handle it. You're an adult. But these people are talking about and judging your child too. They don't want him in their homes. They don't want to go out with him, and they definitely don't understand what he is going through, let alone what you are going through. You've tried so hard to shelter your child from the outside world and the world from your child, that you aren't even sure which way is up anymore. You have spent so much time saying, "Everything is fine," that you don't know how to admit that it isn't, or how to ask for help for yourself.

You know that all of the sacrifices you're making to be there for your child, to be their rock, their foundation, the person they know they can count on and lean on, will be worth it when you both come out of all this and can look back. But right now, that future doesn't even seem possible. You can't picture what life will look like years or even months from now, because living in chaos and turmoil is all you know now. Walking on eggshells around your child comes to you so naturally that you aren't even aware that you are doing it anymore. You spend so much time on the defensive, both inside and outside of your home. You can't remember feeling supported, accepted, or even loved.

I mean, you know intellectually that you have friends

and family who love you, but you've lost touch with what that means or looks like. After all, this is by far the hardest thing you have ever gone through in your life, and it feels like you're going through it alone. There's no one to pat you on the back and tell you what a great job you are doing, that you should keep it up because one day it will get better and life will be great again for both of you.

The Help You Need

You are giving your child that kind of support. But where do you find that support for yourself? Who helps you replenish your energy and helps you see the value in what you are doing? Who reminds you why you keep going through this over and over again?

This book is going to help with exactly that. You will see that I was right where you are, and I made it through with the strategies I am going to show you. I am going to remind you how ugly it has been and how strong you are to have made it this far, and then I am going to give you some tips, strategies, and specific activities to help you make changes. I will show you how I made it through to where I am today.

CHAPTER 2

How Did We Get Here?

Growing up, I was always the "fixer," the person everyone else could count on and turn to for advice or answers. No matter the problem, with a little time and patience, I had always been able to figure out a solution. This made it that much more painful when it began to be obvious that I couldn't fix my son. If I could fix things for everyone else out there—and I truly did think I could do so—then why couldn't I fix the way my son looked at the world around him?

I realize now that this was never about being able to fix anyone or anything, but about being willing to stand with someone in their pain. My life has given me plenty of experience at that. Everything I've been through and everyone I've come into contact with has played a part in forming who and where I am today. Each, in their own way, prepped me for what I was going to need to know in order to go through the chaos of mental illness with my son and hold space for his eventual feeling better about his life.

Things started to change for me the moment I realized that I couldn't fix him or what he was going through or how he looked at life. I couldn't make him want to live, but everything I've ever been through has made me uniquely qualified to go live through this *with* him. You will come to see that you are uniquely prepared to stand beside your child too.

Mental Illness and Other Mayhem

Mental illness was part of my life from the very beginning. My grandmother was schizophrenic, and when I was a young child, my siblings and I we were told to ignore any outrageous or odd behaviour because it was part of her "illness."

Grandma was on monthly needles for her medication. As I got older, I could tell when she'd missed her dose. Although she was a wonderful grandmother to us, when she had missed her medication she would do things that were out of the ordinary. She would get this look in her eyes that all of us can still recognize even in a family photo. Sometimes, when we are reminiscing about my grandma and things she did with us or memories we are sharing, we can all imitate her perfectly. This was part of my fear. Was this going to be how people remembered

Codi? Would this be what people said about him when they share memories?

My parents, aunts, and uncles were all afraid that any of us children would show signs of schizophrenia. I learned to fear it too, for myself and for my own kids. Treatment now is so much different, and we know so much more, but when I was going through the worst of things with my son, the fear that he might be schizophrenic was first and foremost in my mind. It was unthinkable that my son might be diagnosed and then surrounded by ridicule, not only from the outside world, but also from inside his own head.

As I moved into my teen years, I started focusing outside my family. Though I'd had lots of friends in middle school, I chose to go to a completely different high school than they did because I wanted to become a lawyer and didn't want to get distracted from that path. I knew only one person—my best friend—from middle school. The rest of the social scene was filled with so much teenage drama that I was easily able to see that my inner problem-solver's ideal career was helping people in crisis. Since I could see the way to solve things very clearly for everyone else, being a lawyer seemed even more inspired.

But then I ran into considerable teenage drama of my own. When I was 15, I attracted the attention of a 29-year-old man, "Jim." I was flattered that someone so much older was interested in me. He was good-looking, in great shape, and, in my eyes, could have had anyone else—but here he was, looking my way. He drove me to school and picked me up after, asking to secretly spend time with me.

When I was 16, I moved out of my parent's house and in with Jim. Shortly after that, he started making it difficult for me to stay in school. He drove by in case I was outside with my friends to see if there were other guys around me. When I started staying inside during breaks, he was angry with me because he couldn't see me or what I was up to. So I dropped out of school, two credits short of my high school diploma, and started roofing with him. Not an ideal job, especially considering it was unpaid, but I did it because I felt like it was the only thing I was allowed to do that didn't make him mad at me.

I wouldn't learn until years later that his encouraging me to drop out of school and isolate myself from my friends and family were the beginning stages of abuse. At the time, he justified the isolation by telling me my family wouldn't accept us—and he was right. They didn't. So I stopped visiting family and friends who had anything negative to say about my relationship. And that meant everyone.

It wasn't even six months before he started hurting me and threatening to hurt others. Jim told me more than once that he would cut me into one-inch pieces and spread them in the lake. He once threw my dad to the floor to prove to me that he was willing to hurt my parents in order to keep me in line. He terrified me into silence by telling me that he was capable of doing awful things to different family members if I told them what was really going on.

Years of counselling later, I would learn that he was laying the groundwork to make sure I would stay because I would believe I had no other choice. And that's exactly what I did believe. Over the course of the next three years, he beat me quite a number of times. Some attacks left only bruises and scratches; others were more serious. Some of these incidences ended in Jim being taken away in handcuffs and escorted off to jail for various lengths of time. Each time when I phoned the police, I knew I needed to somehow get out of the relationship. One beating was so bad it left me numb from the waist down for three days.

While I was writing this part of my story, my editor asked me to clarify some things for you. She suggested you may be wondering where my family was during this part of my life. The truth is, I can't really answer that because I am not exactly sure myself. I know my parents were aware of what was happening but were unsure how to step in and help without making things worse for me. I felt isolated and alone. When I called home each time Jim was put in jail, my parents always took me back in. But then, when he got out of jail, based on the fear he would hurt my family, I would have to go back with him and the cycle would continue.

What I do know is that eventually, when I knew that I needed help and that I needed to get away from Jim, I was able to call my mom and have a very real and very overdue talk. She suggested I have the same conversation with one of my uncles. I followed her advice and made sure to explain exactly how afraid of Jim I was and that I knew the only way I was going to be able to get away from him was with someone's help. Even though there was police involvement at that time, I didn't feel that it was going to be enough to help me be free of him for good.

My uncle never mentioned that conversation again, and I don't know what happened. But I do know this: from that day forward, I was free of Jim.

Jim had a ton of mental health issues that became growingly obvious even to teenage me. He had a lot of family issues growing up and had lost his mom in his teenage years to suicide. He was also heavily into drugs and alcohol, about which I was incredibly naïve. I didn't even know drugs were a real thing. I thought drugs were marijuana and that everything else was made up for the movies. By the time I realized what was going on and that he was a frequent crack user, I was already too terrified to leave.

I hadn't seen the drug use. I saw issues like anger, depression, controlling behaviour, and anxiety—mental illness issues that were familiar to me, and that all made me want to "fix" Jim. So while it's true I stayed mostly out of fear, I also stayed because I wanted to show him there was a better way to live, that I was loyal and going to stick it out. I thought if he wasn't afraid that he would lose me, like he lost everyone else in his life, then he would change his crazy behaviour.

This is also partly how I felt years later about what was going on with Codi. I knew what it was like to be alone and going through something extremely difficult, and I didn't want that for my son. But I also wanted him to realize that I was there for him no matter what: that I was loyal and going to stick it out through the good and the bad, and that we would figure it out together.

After Jim, I ran pretty much headlong into the man who would become my children's dad. He and I had known each other back when I was 12, living in the same townhouse complex, so when we ran into each other again, he seemed liked a comforting and familiar path out of abuse. Our relationship lasted four years, and we had two boys together, Zachary and Codi, before separating.

I See a Bad Moon Rising

I spent a lot of those years in counselling, coming to terms with the abuse I'd received from Jim, and I'd done a lot of healing. But when Codi, then age 8, first started becoming angry and violent, it took me right back to that abusive relationship. I had vowed that I would never let anyone treat me like that again, nor would I make someone else feel less of themselves based on my actions. This played over and over in my head every time Codi started smashing things or calling me names.

I remember saying to Codi over the years, during

different episodes, that "I was beaten by a man who was 250 pounds, so there isn't anything you can do to me that hasn't already been done." I knew I could not allow my child to treat me in any way that reflected the abusive relationship I was in with Jim, but at the same time, I didn't want to be too hard on him. At the time, I was so afraid of him being schizophrenic, that I wasn't even thinking of the possibility of him growing up to be an abuser.

I told myself that I could put up with the violence and the nasty behaviour because I had taken worse from someone who wasn't my son. If I could do that and survive, I could do this for my son and survive—as long as he wasn't schizophrenic. That, to me, was the worst-case scenario. That would mean he would be like this and going through this for the rest of his life. I replayed in my head all the things my family and my friends had thought and said about my grandma, and I told myself that I couldn't let that happen to my son. I said this to myself like I had some kind of control over a final diagnosis.

But what was simply concerning when Codi was 8 became an issue that consumed us both by the time he was a teenager. Things weren't going so well for Zachary either. While Codi's situation was more extreme, Zachary was getting jumped at school, and both boys were getting bullied and threatened. Eventually, I made the decision to move. I sold my house and moved my boys from Hamilton to St. Catharines. I thought maybe if I got them away from the other kids and the neighbourhood and gave them a fresh start, things would be better. That didn't happen.

Neither of my sons were happy. Their friends and everything they knew were back in Hamilton, so that's where they wanted to be. Once school started, both had attendance issues, but Codi's were extreme. I tried having teachers come to the house to talk to Codi, and even had one teacher offer to buy him Tim Hortons every day he showed up at school.

When bribery failed, I tried calling FACS (Family & Children Services Niagara) to get some help. They told me I was doing everything they would recommend and that the only thing they could do for Codi was counselling if he agreed to it, which he refused to do. He used to tell anyone who suggested therapy that he was not willing to talk to a bunch of people he didn't know and tell them about what he was thinking and feeling. It felt so hopeless! Nothing I was doing was working, and I felt like I was running out of options.

At one point, my boys ran away. They went back to Hamilton, sleeping on friends' couches and staying out all hours of the night. I remember thinking, "Where are these kids' parents and why are they just letting some teenager into their home without even calling me?" At the end of my rope, I filed a report with the police and decided to let them handle it. I also called my doctor for help, who gave me medication to help me sleep at night and concentrate at work.

Zachary ended up moving in with his dad, and then several months later moved in with his aunt and re-enrolling at high school in Hamilton. Weeks later, I got a phone call in the middle of the night to let me know Codi had been picked up by the police and was being brought back home. This wasn't a victory. In fact, this was just the beginning of a string of events that included repeated school probations, violent episodes, police involvement, a set of charges, and, eventually, an overdose and other suicide attempts.

The Healing Crisis

The overdose call came while I was at work. I got a message from my son telling me he was sorry and loved me very much and was so thankful for everything I did, but he made a wrong decision and now wouldn't see me again. My heart stopped. I immediately called Codi's dad and told him that he needed to go find Codi and get him to a hospital. His dad found him and tried to get him to the hospital, but Codi was so out of it and freaking out to the point that his dad pulled over and called an ambulance from the side of the road. Even in the ambulance, they couldn't get Codi calm enough for them to pull away and get him to the hospital. Luckily for him and me, I pulled up shortly after and was able to go in the back of the ambulance to see him and calm him down enough for them to pull away and get him to the hospital.

Each time there was a crisis, Codi seemed to try really

hard to turn things around, but he'd get sucked back into the turmoil and chaos. We tried him living with his dad, and then back with me when that wasn't working for anyone. I sent him to counselling and anger management through probation, which worked for short periods of time—until it didn't. Nothing worked. But I continued to believe that something, somehow, someday, would.

A year went by in a blur and then one day, Codi went off like a tornado in the house. I'm not even sure what was happening or why. He just flipped out and smashed anything in his way. He kicked the back door right off the frame, and then decided to leave. On his way out, he said, "You will never see me again because I'm going to kill myself."

Right after he left, so did I. I didn't want to get caught in the house alone with him if he came back angry. From a parking lot, I called his friends and begged for someone to just tell me he was ok. I just needed to know he was safe. When nobody replied to my messages or answered my calls, I called 911 and the police went looking for him. They told me to come home, which I did, and when I got back to my house the officers were waiting for me both inside and outside my house. They had assessed the damage inside and talked to me about what was going on with Codi.

I explained to them that I felt defeated by the system. I explained that I didn't feel that his problem was a police issue, but I couldn't force Codi to get a mental assessment to see what was going on. By this time, I was sure that this was a mental health issue. I begged the officers to help me get Codi assessed by a doctor. They agreed, talked to him, and took him to St. Catharines General Hospital, where he was admitted and assessed for being a danger to himself. You know how that came out. He was smart, and he got himself released. The next day, he tried to kill himself, and I decided to leave work in a last-ditch attempt to save my son.

We hit rock bottom one morning, a few rough months later, when I woke up and couldn't get out of bed. I was shaking, and my body seemed to go into random mini-convulsions. I was vomiting foam and thought I was going to have a heart attack because my heart was racing so fast.

I was scared, but Codi was terrified. He thought he was going to lose me.

My sister called an ambulance and I was admitted to Niagara Hospital. I spent a whole day there having tests and was finally told my symptoms were stress-related; my body simply couldn't continue to take what was happening around me. When I returned home and told Codi what the doctors had said, this, finally, made a difference. From this point forward, Codi began to turn things around.

He'd been ok with me losing him, but he'd never really considered him losing me. I guess he just always figured I would be here no matter what. Codi started to pay more attention to his outbursts, and I started paying more attention to me. We both realized we couldn't continue the way we'd been going up until this point.

I started to focus on me. I found that woman who'd been through I was going through and knew how to get through it, and I immediately signed up for her life coach and mentoring program. And gradually, little by little, I started to see the light at the end of the tunnel.

More than Just a Mom

As I rediscovered who I was, I found my calling. I started an online coaching business to help give other moms like me a safe place to talk about their struggles with their child and show them they aren't alone. I was determined to help moms of children with mental illness who felt like they were out of options.

I knew telling my story would help others, but I knew I needed to ask Codi if that was ok with him. After all, part of this is his story too. He surprised me when he was supportive, and his answer, then and now, brings me to tears. He said, "If what we went through, or are going through, can help one person—one family—then tell anyone you want."

So, I did. I posted different stories about our journey on Facebook and started to get some interest from others looking for someone to listen and help them. I finally felt like Codi and I were becoming a team. Together, we were sharing what we went through, in order to help others just like us, and it was working.

Eventually I was introduced into Reiki and decided to become a level 1 practitioner. I started offering Reiki and, after a few months, merged my coaching in with this amazing modality. The results were fantastic! I was helping all sorts of people with all sorts of ailments. I was proud of where Codi and I were heading. The Reiki led me into energy work, and then that got me started on working with the MLM (Multi-Level Marketing) community, helping women create thriving businesses so that they can have more time with their families and make more money while staying home.

I knew in my mind that I was helping both sets of people. I mean what better way to stay home with your child who has a mental illness, than to have a business from home. But I just didn't really understand how it all tied together fully. Then the weirdest thing happened. Literally right before I was to write this chapter, I was feeling like I was letting down the moms who have children with mental illness. I ended up bedridden for almost two weeks with crippling sciatic issues. That feeling of not being able to sit or walk or move even a centimeter made me feel physically what I was feeling mentally all those years of trying to help my son.

While I was in bed, trying really hard to figure out what this all meant for me energetically, I realized how many things I was avoiding. The similarities in all the things I went through in my life to bring me right to where I am today. The similarities between the physical feeling of being unable to move and help myself in any way, and the crippling feeling that watching your child suffer from mental illness brings. I realized that no matter how much we try to avoid things, they will always come back at us in a physical way to help us deal with and let go of the stress and emotion we are hiding from. It suddenly struck me that on a very real level, both mentally and energetically, I didn't have to choose between the moms with children of mental illness and the MLM community. I was actually adding to my coaching by giving moms with children of mental illness an avenue to pursue to start setting up a life that works for them and for their child's needs.

Throughout this book, I will show you exactly how I connected the stages of my life with my ability and my strength to get me through all of the deepest and darkest days with Codi's mental illness. I will show you how to tap into your own inner strength so you, too, can move past the struggle and into a new way of life for you and your child.

CHAPTER 3

How This Book Will Help You

Now that you know something about me and the struggles I've faced both in my life and with my son, I will let you in on the journey you and I are going to take together. We will talk, not only about the strategies I found that worked with Codi, but also the behavioural changes I put in place for me. Both will help you get to a healthy and happy place with your child as I did with mine.

Don't be afraid to try these exercises and strategies as you read. You may want to read all the way through and get an idea of where we are going and how, and then come back again and read each chapter one at a time as you make the changes or implement the strategy suggested.

Most of the chapters have some tips or exercises to help you clear out the crap that is no longer serving you and move into the space you need to be in order for the next chapter to work and be as effective for you as it was for me.

I will walk you through each chapter and each strategy and explain what I did and how it worked for me. By the end of this book, you will be able to feel better about where you and your child's relationship is currently, as well as where it is going. You will see that there is hope for your situation and that there is a way to come through all this without feeling like you just have to hold your breath and wait for years to pass or wait for your child to grow out of this. There are different activities for you to do, and although at the time you may not see exactly how it all fits together, trust me when I say, it all comes together. Each exercise is designed to help you clean up different areas of your life in a specific order, so that one day you will look back and realize that your relationship has changed, your house is calmer, and life, if not perfect, is a lot more manageable than it is right now.

Together we are going to dive into mental illness and shine a light into the deepest, darkest parts of your life. You will come out on the other side feeling really good about the changes you have made and about the new life you've discovered for both you and your child. There is peace in this for you, your child, and your relationship together.

So now you are faced with a decision. Do you continue

reading and try the strategies that I am about to teach you? My questions back to you are: What else do you have? Are you tired of living like this? And, more importantly, are you ready to start healing the damage that mental illness has created in your relationship with your child? When I did these exercises, I had nothing else to lose. I only had something to gain. Without movement in some direction, I was terrified I would be burying my son in the near future. I know you know that feeling. It is what drew you to my book.

In the next chapters, you will see that you are not alone out there. There are thousands, if not more, moms just like you and me, looking for the way and the answers to make our child happy again. I have gone through this journey before you, and I can look back to when I was where you are and acknowledge that my son has a mental illness, recognize what was happening back then, and know with every fiber of my being that I needed to do something different. I'm so glad I did.

My son and I were let down by a system that was supposed to know all about what we were going through and what we needed. So I took different things from different sources and different people, and put together this program designed specifically to help you create control within your household. It works. By following the steps, I learned who I was again. I learned how to control me in a way that showed my son how be healthy *with* his illness, not at some future hypothetical point when he might be correctly diagnosed and "cured." Today. as I write this, my life isn't perfect, and my son still has moments, but they now resemble typical teenage moments.

I want you to have this just as I do. My son and I worked on this book together at times, talking about the order things happened or how we each felt. We can now talk about what we went through and reflect on how each of us felt at that time, without arguing! Without blame, or shame, or guilt about what we did or said or how we acted towards each other because we now see how far we each have come. We are both so proud of what we have today.

When looking back over all the things we went through, I asked Codi, "Can you believe it was less than a year ago when our lives were in constant turmoil?" He can only shake his head no. Not even he can wrap his head around how quickly things shifted and changed for us, and how different our lives and our way of life is now, compared to last year. This is what I want for you!

I spent quite a bit of time looking into a number of resources and trying different things that didn't work for me. I am going to save you that trial and error. With this book, you won't have to mess around with the stuff that just doesn't help.

This isn't going to be easy, but it is simple. There is nothing I am going to tell you in the following chapters that you won't be able to implement immediately. If your relationship with your child is anything like mine was, communication has completely broken down. I'm going to give you specific exercises and strategies for opening those lines of communication again. I will help you realize and sort through what is in your control and what isn't. I will show you how to accept the things you cannot change in a way that doesn't feel like you are giving up on your child.

You've got this. And you've got me. Together we are going to change the course of your life and the life of your child.

CHAPTER 4

The Elusive Diagnosis

o you feel like you need a diagnosis in order to move forward?

It feels like it would help, doesn't it? If only you had that one word or phrase—depression, anxiety disorder, PTSD, bipolar—that would sum up all you need to know so you can figure out how to fix it and make it all go away.

But is it really necessary? Do you need a diagnosis before you can make peace with where you and your child are now?

Actually, you don't. While a diagnosis seems like it would make life easier and make everything feel more manageable for you both, the truth is that you can start healing and changing from right where you are.

Just like you, I stayed up late night after night typing

each action, each symptom, and each behaviour into Google. Some of what turned up in search results seemed to make sense and seemed to describe what Codi was going through. But nothing ever really hit the nail right on the head. No single term or diagnosis seemed like a perfect fit. I never got the sense that this was it, that I had found the exact thing I needed to know.

As a matter of fact, I still don't have all the answers even today. Codi has a diagnosis of severe depression and social anxiety, but that still doesn't explain everything we went through and sometimes still go through. I still don't know exactly how to explain the angry outbursts that Codi has. Neither does he.

I tried to explain to almost everyone to whom I was referred for help—doctors, social workers, therapists, and specialists—that although medication calmed Codi's body (too much, actually, he was more like a zombie than a child)—it did little for his anger. He still had angry explosions, going within seconds, from calm and quiet, to completely out of control, swearing, and throwing things. Anger did not appear to be part of his depression or anxiety diagnosis. This was something else. Treating him for extreme depression was not changing his capacity for rage.

The Pieces of the Puzzle

Like you, I did all the "right" things: called the school, talked to social workers and doctors, and took my son to all the recommended appointments to talk to all the people who were supposed to have the answers. But Codi, like all of our kids, is a puzzle, and all those experts just knew one piece of him. The only person who knows the final picture, the only person who holds all of the pieces, is Codi.

I can describe what I see, but I can't describe how he feels, or what the world looks like from his point of view. I only know that at one point, my little boy was joyful and loved life, and in what seemed like the next moment, nothing could make him happy. At times, he still smiled or laughed, but when I looked at his face, in his eyes, I could see that his sparkle was gone.

He used to be a kid whose whole face lit up when he smiled. It was contagious. Looking at him smiling or laughing made you smile and laugh too. Once that was gone, it seemed like his body and mind were taken over by this miserable, crazy being. I knew my little boy was in there somewhere, if only I could figure out a way to find him, help him, and bring him back out.

The one thing that searching Google night after night drummed home to me is that "mental illness" is an umbrella encompassing so many conditions and terms. I began to pick and choose from each category. This symptom fit, but that one or those ones did not. I accumulated a list of things that I knew for sure. He was depressed. He couldn't go into social settings alone. He was angry, very angry. There was no rhyme nor reason why or when things would happen. They just would. One minute we were sitting at the table having dinner, and the next he was losing it.

When I ask Codi now about what this all felt like for him back then, he doesn't really have the answers. All he can say is that he just couldn't control it, and he didn't know it was happening until after. There were many times he couldn't even remember what he had said or done during an outburst.

You Know Your Child Better than Anyone

Looking back now at everything we went through, I've come to see that, although Codi held all the pieces of his puzzle, no one out there in the world—no doctor, social worker, or therapist—knew my child better than I did. You and your child are no different. You know exactly how to read your child. If they have a bad day or a great day, you know it. Even if you don't know the reasons behind your child's behavioural changes, you can see the changes as they are happening.

When Codi and I went to doctor after doctor to figure out what was going on, I was the one who could articulate the changes I was seeing. I was the one telling the doctors everything I could remember about each episode. Codi then would explain how he had felt in that situation, if he could remember or find the words to use. But it always started with me first. I often had to remind him of the specifics for him to be able to get into the nitty gritty of how things were from his perspective.

If you think about it, you are doing the exact same thing right now. Think of the specialist appointments you have been to. They hand you a checklist with questions about your child's behaviour—does your child engage in this behaviour? How often? You are the one filling this out, and it is based solely on your observations and your opinion of how your child has changed. In more ways than you know, *you* are the expert when it comes to your child.

When my client Emily took her son to the specialist's office, she was given a medical form to fill out as well as a questionnaire. She was asked to rate, from 1-10, how often her son displayed any of the behaviours marked on the sheet. Each time she visited the office, she was given the form again to see if anything had changed for either better or worse. Each visit rested on that form, and that form was based on what Emily saw.

When I first took Codi to see a psychiatrist, we had already been through a bunch of parent/teacher conferences and trips to the principal's office due to Codi's fighting, drinking on school grounds, defiance towards a teacher, comments toward other students, and a number of suspensions. I had a general idea where we were heading as far as a diagnosis. There were some things left unexplained, and still are, but overall, I knew my son had anxiety and depression. What I didn't know was how to fix it and make it better.

When people talk about the treatment for anxiety and depression, as well as many other conditions listed under the mental health umbrella, there are a lot of similarities. Diet, exercise, medication, no electronics before bed, and the list goes on. I have tried them all. Well, at least I have *attempted* to try them all. But good luck making a 14-year-old boy do something he doesn't want to do! Each attempt made me feel like I was failing. I was losing the battle and time was running out. I felt as if I was getting further and further away from my son.

Focusing solely on a diagnosis was keeping us stuck. I needed to focus on what we could do to help him, with or without a label for his issues. I felt, as I am sure you do, that if something didn't change, all we were experiencing was going to become the rest of my life. I couldn't possibly do this forever, could I? Could he? We needed change. And fast!

You Know More than You Think

In all honesty, you are already acting without a clear a diagnosis. You go to each of these appointments, speak with doctors, social workers, and specialists, and end up telling them more than they are telling you about your child. You've already been changing things up, trying to find the magic thing that will make a difference for your child. What we're going to focus on in the next couple of chapters is how to change things in your favour—not in the direction your child is taking it.

I remember when Codi was younger, and learning to walk, or ride a bike. He would get up with such confidence, and the look in his eyes was one that said, "I've got this." Then he would get up, and take a step, or peddle a couple times, and over he would go. Of course, as many of us do, I would immediately run over to him, pick him up, brush off his knees, and say something unhelpful like, "Don't cry, it's ok," or, "Ok, that's enough of the bike for today, let's do something else." I thought I was helping, but I wasn't teaching Codi problem-solving skills. We are scared to let our kids fall, but by taking action right away, we aren't allowing them the time to self assess or to figure out what they need to do next.

At the same time as I advocate for allowing our children to work some of this out for themselves, I also have compassion. I think about how I feel after a long, hard day: how I have a hard time coming home and not snapping at the boys or feeling sad for something going on in my life. I try to remember that, even as an adult, I sometimes don't understand my own emotions. I can barely control myself, and at times I can't even do that. And I am not dealing with puberty or mental illness. I try to remember that and have a little more understanding when I am overwhelmed by what Codi is going through. As much as it affects us—and boy, does it affect every single thing we think, feel, and do!—it's so much worse for our child.

You know you will never give up on your child. That's

just not who you are, as much as you think you want to at times. But at times it's tempting to just throw in the towel during the teen years and hope they somehow come out healthy on the other side. Then you realize you aren't ready for that—and may never be ready to make them go through this alone. There is no better time than right now to start taking action toward the peaceful and balanced life waiting for you and your child. Remember, you know more than you think. Here's a quiz to help you learn just how much.

An Exercise

1. I have the ability to recognize that my child is behaving out of character.

    YES   NO

2. If I knew what was going on with my child, I would be able to help him better.

    YES   NO

3. I have already been searching for the answers online based on different behaviour changes I have seen up to now.

    YES   NO

4. I have a rough idea of what diagnosis my child should receive.

    YES   NO

5. I have the strength and determination to help my child understand what they are going through.

    YES   NO

6. I know my child better than anyone else.

    YES   NO

7. I am the best person to support my child so that they can understand, cope, and live with whatever the "diagnosis or answer" is.

    YES   NO

8. I want to help my child through whatever this is.

    YES   NO

9. I am strong enough to be there for my child even if I don't get all the answers.

    YES   NO

10. I am ready for action, even if that means acting without a diagnosis right now.

    YES   NO

Now take a look back at your answers, and you will see that you are ready, right now, just the way you and your child are, for change. You are the person best equipped to help your child get through this, and you are definitely strong enough.

You got this!

CHAPTER 5

When Behaviour is a Choice

When I was younger, we lived in a town-house complex, known here in Canada as a survey. And raising children seemed to be everyone's job. If we were across the survey and did something wrong, whoever saw it, whatever adult that was, came out of their house and gave us trouble. We knew that by the time we got home, our parents would already know the shenanigans we were up to.

By the time I had my boys, that world had disappeared. Instead, I raised my kids in a world where, if I were in the grocery store and one of my kids was crying or having a temper tantrum because I wasn't buying the treat they wanted, people would actually leave the aisle, or even come from another aisle to check out this crazy child and then walk away with a look of disgust on their faces. So many parents judge others with phrases like, "I wouldn't let my child do that," or, "My child would never behave like that." The truth is, none of us really know what we would do or how we would act if or when our child does something until we are actually in that position. More times than not, we do not react the way we thought we would.

Today's world defines both you and your child by your child's behaviour. When your child has a temper tantrum, people start to give you advice about what you should do for your "bad" child. You know your son or daughter isn't bad. You know that inside, they are kind, caring, and loving, and would help anyone. At least, that's who they were before all of the behavioural issues started.

There are times where you still see them in there, but you just need help bringing them back from wherever they disappeared to. Part of the difficulty here, besides not knowing how to help your child, is the shame and embarrassment you carry when you are either out in public or when you are trying to talk to friends or family about what is going on. It's hard sometimes to tell what's worse: worrying about what's going on with your child or worrying about what other people are going to say or think, who they are going to tell, and how they will judge you for how you are handling (or not handling) things.

"Your Son Is Not His Emotions"

None of the doctors I took Codi to see told me this. Instead, I heard this from a counsellor I was seeing to help me take better emotional care of myself. It seemed like such a silly, obvious thing to say, "Your son is not his emotions." I mean, of course he wasn't, and I knew it.

But then I went home, and I thought about that sentence for days. I couldn't seem to forget it or get it out of my mind. I played with this sentence over and over again until one day, I understood it on a deeper level. Codi wasn't a bad child because he made bad choices. He wasn't an angry child just because he had angry outbursts. I thought I had accepted that my son was not his emotions, but truly, I had been judging him just like people in the grocery store. I had been treating him as if he was his behaviour!

So I began labelling his behaviour rather than him. When he had a bad day, whether he was sad or mad, I would say, "Are you *feeling* depressed today?" instead of "Are you depressed?" and, "Are you *feeling* angry or upset?" rather than, "Are you angry or upset?" Each time I did this, I could see the change in his expression. He started to realize, as I had, that he wasn't his emotions: that they were a part of him, but did not define him.

This didn't change his outbursts or minimize them—yet—but it did start to draw awareness to separating him from his feelings. After all, a child who has an angry outburst is not an angry child, they are a child who is crying out for help and using the method they feel is going to get attention the fastest. And if we're honest with ourselves, we have to admit that so far, their methods have worked very effectively in their favour.

Consider your own behaviours, your own reactions, and how you have had a hard time dealing, coping, and controlling yourself. How many times have you said something like, "I am not going to engage in an argument today" to yourself, and then, all of a sudden, you realize you have been arguing with your child for at least 10 minutes? Your first thought is to blame them for making you angry or getting you upset.

That thought right there is my point. You are not an angry person. You are person who gets angry with a situation. Your child is the same. Now is the time to show them and encourage them to own their feelings and their behaviours, and to teach them that those are two different things. You know your child is good inside, you know they have a good heart, and you know they can be happy again. Let's start to separate your child from their anger, their sadness, or their anxiety when they are experiencing it. Then let's separate emotion from behaviour.

From now on, I invite you to start making every effort to include this way of talking to your child in your everyday conversations. Practice saying "feel" before each emotion you are asking or talking to them about. Remember, you struggle with this same issue at times, and your child is full of changing hormones and emotions right now that they don't understand, nor do they know how to deal with them. As you change your thinking and the way you talk to your child, you will separate your child from their emotions and their behaviour.

What is then left is the realization that they can control those emotions and behaviours, even if only sometimes.

Modeling and Teaching Emotional and Behavioural Control

When I started doing this with Codi, I began to see that there were times when he could keep it together, depending on who was around or where we were. For instance, my sister and Codi have a very close relationship, and he doesn't like to upset her—he never has. If my sister was around during a time when Codi would normally freak out, he might make a comment or two (or even tell me to "shut up"), but he wouldn't go into a full-blown episode. Not in front of my sister.

If I had to guess how many episodes she saw of the hundreds Codi experienced, I would say it was less than ten. I bet if you stop right here for a second and think about it, you will be able to come up with someone that your child holds back in front of as well. I started to realize that some of this was choice. Just as I was naming his emotions for him, I started naming this too. I started calling this out for what it was: a choice.

One day Codi and I got into an argument. I can't even remember what about because there are so many arguments behind us. We were in the kitchen, and he was yelling. I was yelling. It was one big, hot mess. He made a comment about me "having" to live this way, telling me that if he had to do so, so did I.

All of a sudden, it hit me. I stopped, looked at him, and with the calmest voice I have probably ever used, I said, "This, right here, is your choice. You choose to yell and scream and fight with me. But this, just so we are clear, is also a choice for *me*. I allow you to yell and scream and fight with me because I feel that it is better than burying my child and never seeing you again."

By this time, I was crying, like ugly crying, in my kitchen, in the middle of what was just the war zone, but I saw a flash in Codi's eyes that told me he knew at that moment exactly what I meant. Without even saying another word, we both walked away from the kitchen, in opposite directions.

There had been many times in the past when Codi told me he was acting out to push me away, so that when he killed himself, I wouldn't hurt. No matter how many times I explained that this wasn't possible, we continued this same dance over and over. By this time, Codi had tried to kill himself several times, and this had finally scared me even more than schizophrenia.

I see now that this kept me living in fear for a very long time. And that fear stopped me from looking for a solution for a long time as well. I just started to accept that this was my life. I hadn't given up on Codi, but I'd given up on myself.

Holding Space for Something Better

By the time I started to work with my coach, I truly believed I had nothing to lose by trying things her way, which meant rediscovering myself just enough to stand up for myself and be able to help Codi trust that, with help, he could and would be able to work things out for himself. It had worked for her and her mentally ill son, so maybe it would work for me. I thought to myself that the worse case scenario was that nothing would change, and it would be just another thing I had tried that had failed. But the best-case scenario was that she knew the way to solve all of this, and I would be able to have a happy and healthy relationship with my son.

I am not really sure I believed things would go in the direction of the best-case scenario. I just figured she would teach me how to manage the struggle better, how to cope with it better than I had been so far. I never dreamed she would be able to give me back my child.

I got some of what she was saying in that moment in my kitchen. I realized that just as Codi was not his emotions or his behaviour, his emotions and behaviour were not always beyond his control. Sometimes, they were made by choice. I needed to learn this—and he needed to learn it too.

Think about life with your child. Have there been times when you've been able to say that you had someone coming over and it was really important to you, and they either stayed in their room, or they were on their best behaviour? Has there been an event, in public, where they were exceptionally well-behaved? Looking back, there were more times like this with Codi than I realized. There were also times when he asked me for something that seemed vitally important (like an Xbox Live membership), and I told him that I'd do it for him if he would do some specific thing for me. No matter what the thing was that he had to do, he managed to get through it just fine.

Sometimes people came over, and he was able to hold it together for an hour here or there. He was able to have a conversation that didn't include excessive use of profanity or feigned ignorance. I started to create these "opportunities" as often as I could. This is important: Instead of getting mad over my discovery that he could control his behaviour far better than I thought, I used it to my advantage. I mean, hey, if he could use it to his advantage, why couldn't I? Plus there was the added bonus that these opportunities and windows of "good" behaviour gave me small glimpses of my child again, the one I knew was still in there. With that came the first little bit of hope that, together, we were going to make it through this.

Mental illness is real, and I'm not saying that your child can just "decide" to be all better. It hasn't worked that way for Codi, and I don't expect that it will. But understand that, just as you are afraid to "lose" the child you know and love to mental illness, they are afraid of being lost as well. Modeling for them that they are strong enough to develop coping strategies and make better choices even within the context of mental health issues is the beginning of helping your child learn to trust themselves again.

An Exercise

Take a couple minutes here and really think about times when your child has been able to hold it together. Write down about five different situations—Christmas dinner, a birthday party, when you had someone over, when they wanted something, etc. If you are on a roll and can think of more than five, stay with it. Really go for it here, because then you are going to look at all that you have written and see if you can find a pattern in these events. Are they all in front of family, or a specific family member? Do they all take place within a similar duration of time? Did your child get something from it?

Really think about and write down these similarities. This will help you when you are planning to incorporate these opportunities into your life more and more.

CHAPTER 6

He's in There Somewhere

Mental illness is like a mask descending over the face of someone you love. You know they're under there somewhere, but it can be hard to see them.

With Codi, I felt like I was on a roller coaster ride, one that I wanted off of, but couldn't seem to get to stop. Then when it did stop briefly, either because he'd made a small gain or because he'd reached out and connected, often in despair, I didn't want to disrupt whatever balance had been achieved. But before I knew it, the ride was going again.

I felt lost and hopeless, trapped in a cycle of being incredibly mad at Codi one minute and then the next minute feeling like my heart was breaking for him. How bad did he have to think life was, I wondered, to feel that not living was his best option? I've been through some pretty rough stuff, and as hopeless as it all seemed at the time, I always felt like there was something more out there for me. Yet here was my child, my son, feeling there was nothing in his life, present or future, that was worth being here for. It breaks my heart, even now, to think that is how he lived for so long.

I know you know that feeling I'm talking about. The one that keeps you searching for the answers because, at this point, anything is better than the thought of burying your child. That possibility is so real right now. You try really hard not to think about it, but it's always in the back of your mind. That thought is always there.

Rage, Shame, Depression, and Back Again

You feel trapped in a nightmare of crazy outbursts followed by extreme lows and sometimes just a flash, a small window, of the child you've been looking for. Even the plateaus feel like the eye of a tornado, not a true place to rest. The nightmare might start again any time, with something as simple as your child asking for a drive, money, or take-out while you are cooking dinner. You say, "No," and then the temper tantrum ensues. The vulgar language begins, the nastiest strain of insults you have ever heard before comes out, things start getting thrown, and for some unknown reason, in a split second it all ends. Your child disappears back into their room.

You take a second to look around and assess the damage. You wonder to yourself what just happened. Then you go into the bathroom or your bedroom and cry. You cry quietly because you want to make sure nobody notices that you've even left. You certainly don't want your child to realize this actually got to you. You emerge from the bathroom or wherever you retreated to moments later and carry on as if nothing has happened. Cleaning up the mess, picking up what's broken and throwing it in the garbage.

Somewhere between an hour and a couple of hours goes by, and your child emerges from their room. His whole demeanor has changed. His face is sad, his eyes are filled with guilt, and he offers to fix or replace what is gone and damaged. Shortly after this come the text messages, apologizing for what was said and done, and then promises that it won't happen again. You have been here so many times before and know this all too well. You know this is the beginning of your child's cycle of self-hate, depression, cutting, and guilt from all the things that he has said and all the things he has done to you. He knows deep down that you are always there for him, and you always will be. So, the guilt, shame, and pain set in and take over your child, for just a little while.

He's still in there. And that's what makes it so unbearable: knowing that the child you adore, the sweet soul with the silly smile, is underneath that mask.

The Eye of the Storm

I remember one day getting a message from Codi out of the blue when he was 16 that said everything I had been waiting years to hear. It was an amazing apology for everything that had ever happened, followed by his acknowledgement that he would be lost without me. It said that he was so thankful that I had been there for him through all of this and that he would feel awful if anything were to ever happen to me. It would devastate him. I was driving at the time I got this message, and I am sure you can imagine how I felt. I cried for days when I thought of that message.

It didn't come at a time when we were fighting or because we'd recently fought, which would make this message simply part of his guilt and shame period. It literally came out of nowhere. I was shocked! Still as I write this out to you, I can't help but get taken right back to that moment and cry. To me it was heartbreaking and awesome all at the same time. I knew he loved me, and I knew he had no doubt how much I loved him. In that moment, it was just a tiny bit easier for me to let go of all that has happened.

The big difference? I knew, in his own words, that he didn't hate me. That's something I wasn't always sure about. I used to joke, when Codi was on medication for his depression and I caught him at the exact right time, that "medicated Codi" would let me hug him. I really liked medicated Codi, and I felt that medicated Codi liked me. Getting this text from Codi gave me the hope and insight that, even without medication, Codi loved and appreciated me throughout this whole process.

That was important for me to know—and it's important for you to know. No matter how vicious the arguments, no matter how violent the acting out, no matter how lost your child seems, he is still in there. And one day, maybe when you're not even expecting it, he will show himself to you.

He's Watching You

You likely feel invisible to your child much of the time. Irrelevant. Ineffective. But he's watching and paying attention to what you are doing. Part of you already knows this because, boy, can kids recall information they need at the blink of an eye if they can use it to their advantage. As soon as they want something, they can quote things you've said to them to plead their case or prove their point. At these times, it's seems like they have perfect recall. This, as much as it seems like nothing right now, or a pain in the butt in the moment, is actually proof that they *do* hear what you are saying, and they *are* watching you throughout this process.

Let's really think about this here. If you know your child is watching and paying attention, what do you want them to see? If what we start to do and model in our behaviour can in any way impact how our child starts to act and behave, then now is the time to really use this skill as a learning tool for them as well as for us. Explore: what can you do in a better way than you are doing right now? It isn't just about how you are dealing with your child. It's also about how you are dealing with work situations or talking about your day at work. Maybe it's about the language you use when talking to your friends or family, or how you talk in general about different situations or people.

Now is the time to really sit back each day and think about how you can change even just one thing in your day. Ask yourself: if you were to see your child in this same situation, how would you want them to react? If you don't want them reacting and acting the way you normally do, consider changing your reaction or behaviour.

This is slightly challenging at first. You don't always think about what you say or do, so this is going to take some time to get used to doing. But even if you start with one reaction or one decision each day, you will find that, before you know it, thinking through your behaviours and making more intentional choices will come more naturally and easily over time.

This cycle of anger filled-outbursts, extreme lows, and the occasional flash of the child you have been looking for can carry on for quite some time. But this, I am happy to tell you, also settles down as your child gains mastery over their emotions and you learn to let go of reactionary responses. I can't say that Codi and I never experience anything like this today, but the outbursts are nothing compared to what they used to be. His sadness is nowhere near as low as it has been. He doesn't cut himself anymore. Suicidal thoughts are now a thing of the past.

I call what we have today "walk-by arguments." These are spurts of arguments about regular, normal, silly things, delivered impatiently as he walks by me on his way to his room. Then, when he gets there, he apologizes for being miserable and explains why he's *feeling* that way. Sometimes it's because he had a bad day at work, or he is sore, or hungry. But he always apologizes and always explains what he was upset about. When Codi and I talk about how things used to be for each of us, we are both so surprised and amazed at how far we have come. We cannot believe the difference in the way we live and the life we have today, compared to how things were for us only just a year ago.

A year seems like it is so far away—and yet when you look back at the year behind you, it seems like just yesterday. One year ago, Codi and I were still living in real hell, every day. A year later, we're enjoying each other's company. We went from instant outbursts where there was no warning, no avoiding them, and definitely no discussions about it all afterwards, to talking every day, laughing together, eating together, and being able to go the beach and have fun out in public. He actually comes to me and asks *me* if I want to do something with him. What a difference a year can make.

It Starts with a Single Step

Your journey out of this chaos is a process, step after step, but it starts here. I've hinted at it when I tell you that your child is always watching and listening. That means you have an opportunity, and a choice. You can react the same old way you've been reacting (if you're like me, that probably means with shock, anger, tears, advice, lecturing, etc.), or you can pause, get a breath, and respond differently in order to get a different result. I know, it sounds impossible, but it's not. In the next chapter, we'll talk about how you can take a huge step toward turning things around just with a single word, or a moment of silence where normally you would have given an opinion.

Once you make the decision to start this first step, you will be surprised by how quickly you see more and more hope in a situation that used to feel and be hopeless.

As you implement each new strategy I am showing you and teaching you in this book, you will be able to see that all it takes is one step in the right direction for things to start to become hopeful again. As you continue to recognize opportunities to separate your child from their behaviour, you will feel more and more confident about the relationship you want with your child becoming a real thing.

At the end of this chapter, I want you to reflect upon different times and situations with your child using the journal prompts that follow. Take your time, but also let the writing happen and don't overthink it. Don't hold back.

An Exercise

- Reflect on an incident with your child. Write out as many details as you can remember. Now, looking back on this, is there something that you could have done differently? If so, rewrite your narrative of this event as if you had.

- Write a letter to your child telling them how you feel. This is an opportunity to say anything and everything you don't feel like you can right now.

- What are you looking forward to the most with your child? Imagine your relationship was different with your child. What does it look like? What is different about it?

- If you could plan a day with your child, without incident, what would that look like? Where would you go and what would you do?

Changing Your Words and Reactions

From the day you found out you were pregnant, you have been getting advice about what to do or not do to, with and for your child. You get advice from strangers in grocery stores and from family and friends. But nobody can give you advice or prepare you for mental illness. Nobody, not even doctors, can give you the exact answer that will make all of this make sense or feel better.

As parents, our instinct is to save and protect our children, to make everything alright for them, and mental illness is an area where we feel like we fail our children on a grand scale. We can't save them from the internal hurt and pain. We can't save them from the conversations going on in their heads. We can't even save them from themselves!

We Can't Save Them, But We Can Help Them

Mental illness covers a broad spectrum of conditions and diagnoses, all with different recommended courses of treatment and management and different prognoses. But there is help, though not a cure, in changing your reaction to and your choice of words with your child. Now that you have started to separate your child from their behaviour, it is time to change your response to what they do and say. In this chapter, we're going to talk about how to communicate differently and even begin to recognize when we might be better off saying nothing at all.

In one of the preceding chapters, I used an example of your child falling off a bike and you running over to brush them off, hug them or kiss them, and try to make it better. We parents do this a lot. We're afraid they'll get hurt. With mental illness, we often try to implement the same unsuccessful strategy. When we see our children creating a situation for themselves (an argument on social media, getting worked up over a video game), it seems very clear to us what needs to be done to fix or avoid that situation. We want to explain this to them so that they can avoid the outcome *we* see coming. We try right away, to step in, offer advice, and to solve the problem before it occurs.

Suddenly, when we find ourselves in the middle of their rage, we are confused about how we got there. It took me a while to realize I *put* myself there. I redirected Codi's anger from whatever he was upset about toward me. By interfering with the process and stepping in, I short-circuited his ability to self-reflect, to problem-solve, and to process any potential consequences. Instead, I gave him an opportunity to unleash all that emotion on me.

Don't Play the Game

Let's think about this for a second. Let's say your child comes to you with some insanely ridiculous problem and is looking for you to agree with their prospective or past actions. You don't agree, and you see flaws or even danger in how they handled or will handle it. You don't want this to blow up on your child and turn into a mental health stressor, so you go into action.

You assume they want your opinion. It is, after all, how the conversation started, "Mom, listen to this, and tell me what you think." But what that sentence actually means is, "Mom, listen and tell me you agree or say nothing because your opinion sucks." You just didn't hear that second part because it was implied, yet unspoken. Then, when your opinion wasn't what they really wanted, you find yourself in the path of their destruction.

You took the decision, the assessment of the situation and its consequences, and the ability to problem-solve out of their hands once again. When you start to hear what they actually meant to say ("Mom, listen, but don't respond if you don't agree with me,") it's easier to stop advising and be the mom who listens to their problems without trying to solve them, then walks away and continues with the day just as it was before that conversation. This won't stop you from playing through what you *could* have said in your head. That will still happen, at least for a little while. But as you learn to listen instead of react, you begin to hold your child accountable for their words and their actions.

When you teach your child that only you can solve their problems, you give them an "in" to blame you when it all goes badly for them (because it does, and it will). In turn, you have made their choices and their consequences *yours*. You have been letting your fear dictate your reaction before you see what decisions or consequences actually happen. You are projecting that fear onto your child and trying to prevent them from having experiences, instead of teaching them that they can handle what comes.

My client Tracey told me about her son Logan who used to go to her constantly about this kid or that kid messaging him on social media, threatening him or "mouthing off" about whatever. To her the situation was simple: just block these kids. If someone messaged you or me on any of our social media accounts and started to threaten us, the answer would be simple: block and delete! Logan, like most kids, didn't get this concept.

Tracey used to just repeat over and over: block and delete; don't engage in such useless conversation. That seemed like an outrageous idea at the time to Logan (and sometimes still does). Back then, Tracey would argue, get upset, and try to warn of the outcomes she saw heading her son's way. She would explain to Logan that people could show up at their house or could try to find Logan on the streets to get into a fight or something worse.

Logan never listened. Usually, somewhere in the middle of the explanation, he'd walk away mockingly reciting the rest of monologue that was about to come out of her mouth. He had heard what she was going to say so many times before.

Then I taught her a new approach. I told her to just listen, and she did: no talking, no commenting, and no offering advice. Logan would finish his story, and she would still be cleaning the kitchen, or doing the dishes. Sometimes he would follow her around the house as she was collecting the laundry and taking it to the laundry room. There were multiple times when she would complete all of these things, and he would still be talking to her. But she would follow the plan and would not respond. Then, when it was her turn to talk, she would say something honest and neutral, and he would look at her as if she just spoke some foreign language he didn't understand.

This was hard for Tracey to do at first. It was hard for me, too, back when I started this with Codi. Giving advice is what I had been doing my whole life: helping people out of their impossible situations, with the simple solution I could easily see. That had become my trademark. That is what I made my business from. I coach women every day, through their seemingly impossible situations, and show them the clarity that comes from changing one thing at a time. Yet here I was with the one person in the world who thought I was the dumbest mother with the stupidest advice and knew absolutely nothing. This turned out to be a great asset for me because I gave him what he was actually asking for: no advice. I started keeping it all to myself.

I want to show you what I mean here, so let's look at Tracey's situation and play it through with differently. Imagine Tracey cleaning her house, and in comes Logan. Logan turns to Tracey and says, "Mom, listen to this," then immediately starts telling her about a situation developing on social media, detailing all the back-and-forth nasty behaviour and the comments between him and the other boy. Tracey patiently waits, continuing to clean the house and collect the laundry. Logan ends with something like, "Don't you think he's an idiot?" or "I should smash him, eh?" Tracey, instead of saying exactly what is on her mind, turns and says, "I'm not sure what to say here, Logan" or "I'm not even going to respond to that," and then walks away.

Eventually two things started happening. The first thing that happened is that he stopped telling Tracey all the social media drama—he realized his mother was no longer going to engage in that kind of conversation. But the other thing that happened is that when he did bring something to her, he was genuinely looking for advice.

Tracey worked steadily to the point where she could ask, "Do you want my real opinion here?" That's the key. Logan, like Codi does and like your child will, knew that if he said "yes," he was going to get an honest opinion, even if it didn't agree with his. I advised Tracey that if Logan said yes, she should give him her opinion—calmly and in a matter of fact manner—and then, when she was done, she should walk away. At first, Logan pushed back, "Ya, but." This was Tracey's cue to disengage immediately.

Ya, But...

Don't fall for the "Ya, but." It is meant to pull you back into the argumentative stage, and you don't want to go back there. If your child says no, which they will, 99 percent of the time, just smile and say, "Okay, no problem."

This is actually just as good, if not better, than your child saying yes. When Codi told me that he didn't want my advice, I knew that he already had figured out what I was going to say. It was right there at the front of his brain. I knew that the second he said no, my words were already playing in his head, because he would walk away. I considered this new strategy a win for me because no matter what answer came out of his mouth, my words, my advice were there for him either way.

Changing your reaction to and the way you talk to your child are two separate strategies combined to make one really effective tool. When you stop reacting to your child the second you hear their problem and you stop giving advice every time they come to you, you create space for change. When you start to say things like, "I don't know," instead of blasting them with what you do know, they stop coming to you. They stop asking you. They know you *do* know. They know you are dying inside to just tell them, but they've also learned that you won't tell them unless they say yes—until you make them take responsibility for receiving advice.

You may be wondering right now how this can be a good thing. After all, you want your child to come to you and tell you what's going on in their lives, right? My answer is both yes and no. You want to know what is going on, and you want them to come to you. But right now, they are only coming to tell you all the drama and all the stuff they know will get you going and start an argument you really don't want to have. You're caught here between wanting to know what's going on so you can "help" them, and them not really wanting your help—they just want to argue.

With this tool, you will hear less about the drama and more about your child. You will know that when your child does, in fact, come to you with a problem, they have actually thought it through. They have played out in their head all the potential things you could say, and now they truly want your advice. They aren't trying to argue.

Sometimes Codi still comes to me with something I consider resolvable with an easy fix or solution, and at those times, it seems like the advice is just sitting on the tip of my tongue. Because we have come so far, sometimes it even slips out before I realize what is happening. It is easy to forget that he still really doesn't want me to "fix" things for him. He just wants me to listen. Listening instead of reacting takes practise, but it's a constantly evolving tool that will make a big difference as your relationship progresses toward healthy communication.

You can apply this to your other relationships and friendships too, because we adults sometimes do the same thing. Think about a time when you've come home from work, or are out with friends or family, or have just talked to someone on the phone, and you turn to your significant other and complain about what just happened. You don't want them to "solve" your problem, you just want an ear. If you are honest here, you even do it when it comes to your child. You have an argument with them, and then call someone, whoever you have that you can confide in, and you start telling them what happened and what you think about it all. What you are looking for is just someone to listen to you, someone to agree with you. What you get, though, is someone who doesn't have a child who is going through all this. They start telling you what you should have done or what you should do now. When you hang up, you are more frustrated than you were when you started the conversation. Sometimes, you actually end up arguing with the person you just called before you hang up. You see, we don't like unwanted advice either. Why do we then assume our children want it given to them?

The peace that comes from refraining from giving advice benefits both of you. Right now, your child only comes to you because they are angry and want the confrontation. They want to release the anger and frustration or hurt that they don't even know they feel, and when we engage, it's the perfect opportunity for them. They release that emotion and are able to go back to their room, outside with friends, or simply just carry on with their day as if nothing has even happened. Here you are, all bent out of shape, stewing about what could happen, what just did happen, and replaying it all in your head, going over all the things you should have said but didn't think about at the time. Your day has officially been ruined.

When you stop engaging in the unhealthy advice giving and only give advice when they ask for it, you change the overall feel of the communication you have with your child. Right now, you cringe every time they come to you because you know what is going to happen. No matter what they say, you are going to disagree or get upset about what they tell you and then, for the rest of the day or for the next couple hours at the very least, you give each other the silent treatment. That's if you're lucky and things don't escalate into a full-blown yelling, screaming, and throwing stuff kind of argument.

Forgive Yourself for Slipping Up

Making this change won't happen overnight. It will take time to perfect this method. However, once you do, it will be a solid building block to get back to a time when your life seemed normal and seemed to make sense to you. I still work on this one. Sometimes I still struggle with it. It is a lifelong process to master this method, but you will see results instantly here, and because you do, you will know you are on the right path. It becomes easier to catch yourself when you slip up, and it becomes so much easier to fix. The second you feel advice slip out of your mouth, your brain will start to tell you to stop talking. Sometimes, I have stopped mid-sentence. At those times, Codi would ask me to finish, and I would just say it was nothing and not important, or that I had completely forgotten what I was going to say. He knew this wasn't true. He knew that I knew exactly what I was going to say, but that I wouldn't play. That left him with only one option: walk away.

Once you start this technique, you may see your child testing you at first. Don't give up and don't stop trying. It will start to work. Your child just wants to see if you are going to be consistent at this. So be consistent. You have so much strength inside you waiting to come out, waiting to reclaim your life. You have made it through some pretty awful things, things you don't even speak about because you don't want others to know what goes on in your home. Trust me when I say that I know exactly what you are going through. I know exactly where you are right now, and I am telling you exactly how I got to where I am with my son today.

This is where it all begins. Believing in yourself, standing in your power, and remembering you're not alone here. In a situation filled with noise and drama, silence is powerful. It is a step in the right direction. I look back now, and I realize I had no idea all those years before, that this would be so effective. The truth is, I had become so wrapped up in my son's world, I couldn't see a way out—just like you have been feeling. This is the start of the way out!

What's Left to Talk About?

It might seem like, if you take away the arguing and the unwanted advice, you won't have much left to talk about. So that's what we are going to build on next. I am going to show you how I figured out what to talk about, and you are going to learn what I did to change the communication from always fighting to having healthy conversations with Codi. We both can tell now, very early on, if things are going to take a wrong turn, and one of the two us will abort the conversation. The other is grateful and respects the healthy boundaries we have established.

Now I realize that this sounds too good to be true. It also sounds like I am saying Codi and I don't ever argue. We do. The difference is that now it never gets hostile like it used to. It is never an argument that ends with things being broken. Codi and I are able to talk 95 percent of the time in a way that leaves us both feeling better about our relationship and our communication skills.

To start this, you are going to start listening to how your child talks to other people. I spent so much time trying to avoid talking to Codi that, when I eliminated most of our arguments, I had no idea what to say to him. I started listening to things he talked about with other people. I would pay attention to shows he was watching or things he said to my family when they asked him how things were going with him. Since Codi and my sister were always close, this is a big part of where I started to learn about my son. Listening to questions others asked, then when we were home, just he and I, I would ask a similar question or a question about a topic I heard him talking about.

It is partially trial and error here. There are going to be some things you try to ask, like how their day is going, that may turn into an argument. Don't get discouraged. There will be some fail- safe subjects that come up. You will learn more about your child from listening to others with them, and then you can use those topics or those conversation starters when you want to start talking to your child.

You see, so far you have a very unhealthy relationship with your child. You have to rediscover your child, and they have to rediscover you. You have to reteach them how to talk to you, and it starts by using easy topics like movies or food. Sometimes you will already know what your child is going to say. I remember listening to my sister talk to Codi, or listening to my 2 boys talk, and then later or the next day I would repeat the information as if I didn't know he already answered the questions or knew the story. But what it did for us: it taught us how to be kind to one another. We developed similar likes, or at least we started to realize we had things in common.

For this chapter you are going to write out a list of your child's behaviours and triggers. I will give you some examples to get you started. This is going to start you off at being able to recognize your child's behaviours and eliminate some the triggers to allow you to stop the arguing. This step will put you back at square one with the communication between you and your child.

An Exercise

Behaviours	Triggers	New approach
Yelling	Offering my opinion	Keep my opinions to myself
Throwing things	Arguing with my child	Walk away when it becomes argumentative

Now take a look at this list, and start with the triggers. When one of the "opportunities" in the Triggers column comes up, note it, and start eliminating it from your relationship. Of course, if they are necessary, then so be it, but for now we are going to try to eliminate most of these situations. When we take the trigger away, and replace it with the new approach, we change their behaviour.

This may be difficult at first because right now you are probably arguing with your child multiple times a day, so it is not going to stop in a day. But if each day you stop one argument and the next day two and so on, eventually you will look back and see that your days have hours of peace in them. Can you remember the last time you went from breakfast to lunch, or lunch to dinner without an argument?

I suggest that you make a chart and use it to fill out with the topics that actually work with your child. When you discover a topic or a new conversation opener that works, keep track of it here. Then, when you are having a day where you feel like you are going backward—and that will happen—you'll have this chart to not only show you that you can do it, but to give you actual conversation starters to get you back on track.

CHAPTER 8

He's Stepping Out of Isolation

L et's take a look at how far you have come. You started with the realization that you don't need to know exactly what is going on with your child. You don't need a label for you to move forward and start working towards the life you want for you and your child. Then you began to see your child separately from their emotions. You realized that you, yourself, struggle to figure it all out after a bad day. That we all direct our emotions at the wrong people sometimes. Your child does too.

Then you changed your language. You started saying they "feel" instead of they "are." You recognized when your child was feeling angry or upset and when they were acting based on your reactions. You now understand that, yes, some of this just "happens" before they realize what's going on, but some of this, if not most of this, is a choice they are making. They are choosing to live in anger and hurt because they don't understand that is a decision they are making. When you see it first, they can too. When you choose your words, your steps, and your direction, they will start doing so as well. You have learned that you can teach them exactly how you want to communicate with them. That will happen. They don't know where your relationship is going—and, honestly, neither do you at times—but they will follow your lead.

Inside, your child is craving a healthier life and a better, more effective way to communicate too. They want all of this to make sense just as much as you do. They want to be able to get through the chaos and back to a time when life was simple and fun. They just have no idea where to start or how to start. As you implement each of the strategies here in this book, you are showing them the way. You are going to look back years from now, while you are sitting with your child and having fun or watching a movie, and remember the times when you thought having fun was never going to happen again. It will seem like it was forever ago.

Getting Outside

Now it's time to get out of the house. It's time to start making plans and sticking to them. It's time to invite people over. You will take baby steps here, an hour here or there, perhaps just a walk around the block. But it's time to let the outside world in.

I know that this sounds scary. The thought of letting others see what goes on in your house and with your child is extremely scary. His behaviour is embarrassing at best. You play each incident over and over in your head filled with guilt and shame for each thing said or done. You know you didn't do this to your child, but there are still times when you wonder where you went wrong. The thought of inviting others in, to let them see that, is probably making you cringe right now. Believe me when I tell you, I get it. I understand that feeling completely.

You have two very different fears here. One is attached to letting people in. Letting people see what it's really like. You're afraid of the judgment, and you are also worried about how people will react if or when your child acts out. The other fear is attached to leaving your child alone in the house. What if something happens, to them or your home? What if someone comes over? What if your child needs you? These fears have driven your thoughts and behaviour so far, and understandably so. Up until now, things have been a mess in your house and in your relationship with your child. Your fears seem completely justified by your child's actions so far.

It is, however, just as important for your own sanity as it is to your relationship with your child, to get out of the house and/or let people in. This is going to be where you start to feel, even for a small amount of time, that you can have a normal life. You can have people over for a tea, or to sit on the porch and just talk about whatever new thing is happening in their lives. You can go and watch a friend's son play football, even if it's just for an hour or so. You will start to feel like you can breathe again. You will see that not all of what is going on in your life is bad or dramatic. There are moments and opportunities for you to reclaim your life outside of who you and your child have become.

Before now, you may have made plans to go for coffee with that friend you haven't seen in months, or for a walk with a family member—but you cancelled. You didn't go. Your child was having a bad day, or a temper tantrum, or just hiding in their room wanting to be alone, but not alone in the house. You have lived in fear of what would happen if you left the house, even for a second, for far too long now.

The Best-Laid Plans

I remember making plans with a girlfriend of mine to go for coffee. She was going to be in the area with her son at a football practice. I remember the day exactly. We made plans days before, and I prepared Codi in advance. I told him that I was going out for an hour. I even told him who I was going with, because he liked this friend. The day came, and he was having a good day. He was calm and quiet, playing a video game most of the day with no chaos whatsoever. I was on edge all day wondering if I really going to make it out of the house. I was in full antic- ipation mode of this not happening. I worried about what I would say; what excuse I would use; how I would get out of this one. I probably looked at my phone to check how much time I had more than 100 times throughout the day. I even thought of cancelling a couple of times, so I didn't have to cancel at the last minute. When crunch time came, and I needed to get ready to go, I did. I brushed my hair and brushed my teeth. I put on deodorant. I called down to Codi to tell him I was heading out to meet up with my friend.

And just like that, he was not ok with me going. Suddenly he was waiting to do something with me, and now I was going out. What was he going to do? The guilt set in. How could I possibly be going out and leaving my son here when, finally, he wanted to do something with me? He was waiting for me all day! I started to rethink things. Was I avoiding him all day? What option did I have at this point? I had to cancel—or at least I thought I did. I messaged my friend and bowed out. My friend texted that she understood, and I felt relief, like I had gotten myself off the hook. But I also felt like I was letting myself down.

I *was* letting myself down. For the next few hours, I tried to make plans with Codi, but he wanted no part of it. I sat in my chair, looking out the window and regretting my choice for the rest of the night.

I'm sure this story sounds familiar. You've probably done something like this many times yourself. Our kids aren't trying to be mean; they often don't even realize their impact on us. To them, we're like a security blanket. They don't want us in their rooms and in their faces, but they sort of want us around for comfort, or in case they get bored. I truly don't believe they do it on purpose, at least not for the most part.

Bringing the Outside World In

Today is the day it all changes. Today is the day you reach out and make plans again. You are going to call that friend and invite them over. You can explain that you only have an hour of free time, or that if they are coming over, they might see some sort of craziness from your child, but you are going to make plans anyway.

Up until now, you've only made plans with those people you knew would understand when you cancelled five minutes before you were set to meet. They were your safety net. But today is day you move the safety net to the side. It's still there in case you genuinely need it, which will make you feel comfortable, but you are going to truly try not to use it, which will make you uncomfortable. Don't give in. You need this.

If you think about it, your child mostly engages in his worst behaviour in front of you and you alone. Even when it is in public, it is all about you. You know the times when you dragged your child out, trying to show them they have to listen to you, and then suddenly you find yourself regretting that decision? Your child is mid-incident. It feels out of control, but it isn't. They are doing it to get you to go home or give them something they want. They don't see any of the people, they only see you and your reaction to them *because* of the people around you. They realize they can get what they want. They have been using this method, really, since they were young.

But the reality here is that when you bring people into your home, you limit the audience factor. When your child is at home, doing their own thing, the chances of an incident decreases. It's not completely gone, which is why you are going to start with small visits. You are going to slowly increase the time so that your child doesn't flip out, and so you can also get comfortable with having people over. If I were to tell you right now to set up a family gathering for a full day on Saturday, you'd shut this book and think I was completely nuts! But with practise and time, you will get there.

Let's think about this. You probably have a friend like mine who understands when you cancel an outing at the last minute. Don't you think she'll understand if you have to cut coffee short at your house, or if something ends up happening? The truth is that she will, and you know it. So what's holding you back? Just fear. Fear of what you have been hiding for so long coming out. Fear of what other people will think of your child, or you. You have lived in fear long enough. Now it's time to put fear to one side and start making plans.

Baby Steps

Remember: start small with a coffee or a walk. The important thing here is to stick to your plans. That is the key: sticking to plans and not cancelling. Of course, if there's an emergency and you truly need to cancel, then cancel. You will know when it is a true emergency vs. an emergency your child (or your fear) is making up. But if your child "wants to do something with you" or "doesn't want to be alone," then I challenge you to go. I challenge you to stick to your plans.

You will start by trying to talk yourself out of it. You will run through all of the what-ifs in your mind. When this happens, and it will, ask yourself, is this fear? What am I afraid of right now? Am I afraid of something going wrong, or am I afraid of the possibility that my child is actually going to be fine without me for an hour? You have become so involved in your child's mental illness, and the way *they* have shown you to live, that you believe you *need* to be needed by them. This way of life has completely snuck up on you. The thought that they don't need you is scarier than anything you have gone through or can think of going through right now. Understand one thing though: even as adults, even as "normal" kids, they are always going to need you.

Now, it wasn't obvious to me, and I'm going to assume it's not obvious to you, that part of healing is starting to talk about your life. People *do* need to know what we are going through. People *do* need to see what this is like for all of us who deal with mental illness. The truth is, not only are you tired of hiding and lying about it, but you also need to know you aren't alone in this. When I started to talk about what was going on in my house and with my son, that is really when I realized how many others are just like us. There are so many other moms going through the exact same thing you are, but you will never know and never see that if you are hiding in the closet in fear of the unknown world of mental illness.

When I started talking and sharing my story and my struggles with those around me, I also realized their reaction wasn't what I expected. Not even close to how I imagined it in my head. I mean, sure, there are some people out there who will judge both you and your child. You can't stop that, nor can you control it. But you will see, as I did, that your family and your friends are all worried about you and your child. They're concerned, and like you, they don't know what to do or how to help. My support through this ended up coming not from within me, but from the outside world. It came from others who were just like me, people had a child with mental illness and knew what I was going through.

Letting Go of Shame

The one really big thing I learned during this stage of my "recovery" was that people could only judge me for what they didn't know or understand, or what I was ashamed of. When you stop being ashamed of your life, and you start owning it because it's yours. People's opinions and judgments don't matter. This might seem far-fetched, but it's so freeing when it happens. People who judge don't get it, and really, we don't want them to. This is awful to go through and awful to wake up to day after day. We wouldn't have volunteered for this life, this challenge, and yet here we are.

When people start to judge, just know that deep down inside, they don't get it, so their opinion doesn't actually have substance. Only those who have a child with mental illness will get every single thing you say, and they won't judge because they do understand. We are all in this together. We are at different stages, and we don't know that each other even exists right now. But that is why talking about it is so important. Today, I know I have a group of loving and amazing friends, who know *exactly* what I am going through, and what I have come out of, and that makes all of what I had to do to get here so worth it. What I am trying to tell you is don't worry about other people and their judgment. It isn't a reflection of you, or your life, or your child. It *is* a reflection of them!

I soon started to realize as I started opening up, just how many others also felt alone. I realized how much strength I actually had, and with that strength, I decided it was time to talk to a bigger crowd, so I could help more people just like me who were dealing with a child's mental illness.

So here you are. Now the only thing left to do is talk about it. Stop hiding your reality, your truth. Give what you are going through a voice. Give it a chance to exist and be acknowledged. I know it's scary, and when I say scary, I mean absolutely terrifying to you right now. It may feel like a huge risk, but trust me when I say that only through your acceptance and your acknowledgement of where you are can you be free. This is the way for you to be able to come out, have coffee, see a movie, or spend a day with your friends on the beach without a cloud of chaos following you everywhere you go.

Right now, it may seem like these things are out of your reach, like they don't even exist in the possibilities you see for yourself and your future. But trust me, they exist, they are possible, and they are waiting just at your fingertips for you to grab hold.

All it will take is that first step forward. You may even find that dealing with all this, all that happens behind closed doors, becomes so much easier to deal with as soon as you start talking about it. When you know that you aren't alone, that there are others in your city, in your neighbourhood, or on your block who are going through this too, you will find it so much easier to talk about. Before you know you will be telling everyone who asks. When people say, "I haven't seen you in forever," you will be able to say why without guilt or shame.

You will also be so surprised at how sympathetic people are. In your mind right now, you imagine that people only think two things: you are a bad mom, and your child is bad too. Once you are out and talking, you will see you are a great mom. You are willing to do anything for your child—and you have. Your child is great too. He or she may be going through difficult stuff right now, but they are still great. They still have an amazing heart, and they want just as badly as you to be accepted and loved for who they are, even when they aren't having a good day.

For our end-of-chapter exercise, I invite you to make a list of people who you can start making plans with, either by inviting them over, or by asking them to do something outside the house with you. Make a second list of things you can do to get out of the house. It doesn't have to be a big list—here's a small chart to get started. Feel free to add to it as your list and time outside the house grows.

An Exercise

People You Want to Make Plans With	Places You Can Go to Get Out of the House

CHAPTER 9

Your Stories Are in Play

Think back to a time before your child, to a time when *you* were a child. That's where things really began for you. Childhood is where we all develop who we are and who we are going to become. This is where we develop our belief system and our core values. This is where we start to learn what is expected of us and, through trial and error, create a way of dealing with the world around us. As a child, we don't yet realize the impact of our decisions, but as an adult, we start to realize and acknowledge that all of the things that happen to us really happen *for* us. Sound hard to believe? It's true. This is what sets us up to become exactly who we are today.

Who Are You?

Who exactly is that? Who were you? Who have you become? You may not be sure of the answers right now and, if you are, you may not feel those answers are good ones. But I am about to show you that everything you've gone through has made you into the amazing woman you are today. You are strong, you are a survivor, and you will not let anything stop you from succeeding in your life. Deep down, you know this is true. So own that. Sit with it for as long as you need for it to really sink in. Really acknowledge it deep down so you can say it yourself every day.

Look at how far you have come. Look at everything you have come through. You're here, still fighting, still being you, and still being awesome. Nobody, not even your child, can take that away from you. You have that instinct that tells you that you are going to get through this, even when you're not sure you have it in you. I am here to tell you that you do!

I had a great childhood, full of fun and filled with family. My mom was one of ten—that's right, ten. My dad was one of seven, and most of my aunts and uncles had two or more children. So when I say I have a big family, I mean it. Plus, we were all really close. My parents grew up together—literally. They lived on the same street and all hung out together, my mom's family and my dad's family. They had me when they were young, and so I became a child of their group of friends. I have "uncles" who have been there with me my whole life, purely by choice, because they were best friends with my parents when I was born.

We had the type of home where everyone stopped in.

You didn't need to call, you just showed up. No matter what my mom made for dinner, there was always enough for whoever walked through the door. It is probably the thing I value the most to this day. I love that my family was so close and always seemed to be together. Big Christmases, big dinners on Sundays, and just because. It was a great way to grow up.

Boundaries? What Boundaries?

But no matter how good I had it growing up, there's the unavoidable fact that I made some really bad decisions—like dating a 30-year-old man when I was 16. I realize now that all that family togetherness was great, but I never really developed any boundaries, which was one of the reasons setting them became so important when I was struggling to adjust to parenting a child with mental illness.

Not only did I have poor boundaries, I also felt I had no right to complain. My parents weren't perfect, but they did everything they could think of to make sure we had a great childhood. When my siblings and I looked around, we saw the difference between our childhoods and others, and we saw that others definitely had it worse.

"I have no right to complain because other people have it worse," was a story I told myself for years. Even when I was being beaten, I thought to myself that it could have been worse. It wasn't like I was hospitalized or had my face distorted. I used this justification to stay in that relationship, and the relationships that followed—and there were plenty—fell into the same category: "This isn't so bad; others have it worse."

I also had an underlying belief that relationships are hard work, and that most people just weren't willing to stick it out. There's truth there, perhaps, but boy, did I take endurance to a whole new level. I stuck it out through years of abuse. Then I was cheated on and still thought I could "fix" him because someone, somewhere, had it worse, and I was not giving up.

Now think about how your own childhood and how your upbringing affects your relationship with your child. Think about your story, your life. Really think about your friendships, your jobs, and your relationships. Think about how they all prepared you, positively and negatively, for this moment right now. You likely have poorly defined boundaries with your child. You may also be like me and think there is a family out there who definitely has it worse than you, and you are just hoping and waiting for the day when you child wakes up and sees this, then they will come out of this struggle with an immense appreciation of everything you did for them. You can't wait for them to see how you stood by them! That moment right there, that is going to make the last couple years of your life worth it.

Really think about this. Your child does whatever they want and whenever they want, for the most part. They aren't thinking of you here. They aren't wondering what you feel or think when you are patching that ginormous hole in the wall, again. They aren't cancelling plans to stay home with you when you are having a bad day, but you do it for them. They say things to you that you would never allow from anyone else, things you would never say to them or others. But a minute later, when they are calm, you forgive them. You try to forget the incident even happened. You've learned not bring it up again, because you definitely don't want a repeat of that!

It's Not So Bad, Right?

You tell yourself you are doing this *for* your child because the situation *could* be worse—and to you, it could be. At first, I told myself at least Codi wasn't suicidal. Then, when he was, I told myself that at least he hadn't succeeded. Like me, you may have it in your mind that other moms must have it worse, they must go through more. You may think that others definitely have it really rough, because what we are going through has to be more manageable than those who have had to bury their child. In fact, everyone in every system you've talked to has probably told you exactly that.

Each referral, each denial of treatment, has come with the words, "Your child isn't bad enough"—yet—to make the emergency list. They aren't "bad enough" to bypass the six-month waiting list that exists in every specialist's office. You have been told that there are other children out there who *want* the help, so they deserve the help and the spot more than your child. These sentences are ringing through your head, in all the voices of the people who said them, over and over again. Without realizing it, these are the things that keep you going around and around this vicious circle of your child's mental illness.

The idea that "other people have it worse" doesn't, however, tend to increase our appreciation for what we have, nor our belief in our ability to turn things around. Parenting a child with mental illness is stressful, and sometimes, it's really hard to see anything positive in it or that will ever come from it.

Finding the Gifts in the Grit

What is it about your current or past experience that is perfect for you? When I take off the negative glasses through which I once viewed the world, I can see that I have a great family who loves me, no matter what. They will always be there when I need them. They will always be willing to move past the silly thing that happened, whether it was mine or theirs—it doesn't matter. They are always just a phone call away.

I can see how the abusive relationship helped give me inner strength and a willingness to be transparent: I am completely ready, willing, and able to talk about what goes on in my life because the way I see it while I am going through it, isn't the same as others see it, no matter how much I tell myself that's true.

I can now see how the cheating and the craziness

that followed on my subsequent relationships gave me the strength to create boundaries and enforce those boundaries. It helped me see my true self worth, and that relationships aren't just about sticking it out waiting for the one day when someone notices you are there. I have learned, through my life, that relationships are about accepting each other for right where each of you are in the moment. That means two people have to be in it, and two people have to be happy, not just one. With each new relationship, I demanded a new way in how I wanted to be treated. I let go of one of the things I didn't like from the last relationship. I grew stronger and stronger, knowing more and more of what I liked and didn't, and what I wanted and what I didn't. I became exactly who I was supposed to be, exactly who I am today.

When you do this, when you look at all you have been through—and I recommend you do it soon—you will see you are able to connect the dots, from where you were at each stage, to where you are right now. You may find it easier to write it all down, to make a list for yourself. You may need to see it down on paper. You know it in your head, but in your mind it is so easy to put each one aside on the way to looking at the next one. When it is on paper, you can look at everything as a whole, and you can see the entire big picture of your life. Then you can see how each event or each person set you up to be ready for where you were going next.

This is where releasing the past, releasing the fear, and

stepping into who you are starts. Right now, we are the ones who keep ourselves right where we are. As much as we want out, and we do, we are the ones who have locked the doors, shut the windows, and made sure all the blinds are closed so the sun can't come in and, unfortunately, we can't see out. By putting it all down on paper, by looking at it, and looking for the positive lesson that came out of that negative situation, you can find the sunshine.

When you have done this work, take a really good look. Your experiences describe you! They describe someone who has been through enough to justify hiding and mistrust. They describe someone who wants to shut the whole world out. But on the other side, next to that list of unfortunate experience, you also have a column of the amazing stuff you've learned. Amazing strengths that have taught you exactly what you are made of and who you are. You can confidently look at this list and know without any doubt that you are ready right now to open the blinds, open the windows, and, for the love of all things, ready to unlock the door and live the amazing life that is waiting for you just on the other side of that door.

You are ready for this. It is real, and it is waiting for you. I am proof. I opened that door and now, I am so thankful I did. You are ready to sit with your past, and assess it, recognize it, and look back at it with such amazement for how far you have come. Think of it like clearing out your closet. When spring comes, we look at all the clothes in the closet that we haven't worn in years and what doesn't fit us anymore. Then we bag it all up and donate it or give it away. Think of this like that. When you have it all down on paper and can see what courage and strength you have, you are ready to let it go. Let it be exactly what it is, the past.

All of this has helped you get here, but there's no reason to hang onto it. Lovingly let it go. Release it, and know that you, today, have the confidence and the power to get through anything. Nothing has stopped you from getting this far. So face it, you aren't about to let anything hold you back now. Don't hold onto the negativity of it all. Allow your child to live their life, with you right there watching them, so that their hardships will help them learn lessons, build character, and develop strengths, just the way your past has helped you.

Here is where you make that happen. Write it down in point form if it helps. It doesn't all have to be in order, you just have to be able to look at it all together when you are done. This will give you a big, clear idea of how far you have come and how strong you really are. I think we lose that along the way when we focus only on the one incident or event we are dealing with at the time. But when you are able to see, without reliving, what you have gone through to be exactly where you are today, you are able to understand that you are strong and you are enough. You are perfect and ready just the way you are, right now, to be happy.

CHAPTER 10

Filling Your Cup

In the preceding pages, you've taken a look at what's going on around you. You've dug deep into your past and opened your eyes to exactly what you have been hiding from so that you can let it go, with love. Now, there is one big question left to answer:

Who are you besides your child's mom?

You may not even know that anymore. Most of us become so consumed with being there for our child that we've lost touch with who we are. This is the time to find out. You've gone for far too long not knowing. Claiming who you are may take some time, but I know you can do this.

50 Things You Like: An Exercise

Get a notebook or a piece of paper and write a list of 50 things you like. There is no wrong answer here. If you can think of it, you can write it. The only catch here is that it has to be something you *genuinely* like (a favorite activity, for example) and not something you think you *should* like.

When I first tried this, it took me almost a week to get something down on paper. I couldn't even think of a single thing. I thought of lots of things I thought I liked, but then when I asked myself if I actually liked it, or if I was doing it for someone else, I got stuck. I had to really think about who I was doing these things for.

For instance, for a couple of years, I drove in demolition derbies. I loved it. It made me nervous, but I got such a thrill from it. I wrote it on my paper as one of my things. When I thought about it, I realized driving in demolition derbies wasn't what I loved. I loved the environment, and I loved that I did it as part of the relationship I was in, but when I was honest with myself, I realized that if I weren't in that relationship, I wouldn't do it again. I also wouldn't have tried it in the first place. So, I took that off my list. I then went back through my list, and I ended up eliminating everything except one item. I can't even remember what that one thing was now. But I do remember that once I figured out what I was doing for me and what I was doing for others, it was actually easier to identify what I liked.

I learned one big thing about myself from this list: I love doing kid-like things, like mini-golf and arcades. I thoroughly enjoy arcades! I love playing. Lying in the grass and rolling down the hill, like I did when I was a kid. That kind of stuff. I didn't know that about me before this exercise. Since then, I've discovered so many things I like, just by thinking of things I had been doing or things I wanted to do. I listened to others talk about things they were doing and liked. I would try them out or say to myself, "Oh, I like that too." Now, I could write a list for days of things I like. Really, I could add "making lists" to the list of things I like, because I do like to make lists. I like to be organized.

Remember, you don't need to do this in one go. Just start your list, remember it exists, and remember where you put it. One day, when you're making dinner and dancing in the kitchen, you'll remember how much you love to dance and then you can add it to your list. The important part of this is that you keep adding to it and that you add only things that are your likes. I will explain how your list will help you by the end of this chapter.

Your Perfect Day: An Exercise

Next, let's start daydreaming. What does a perfect day look like for you? Are you alone? Are you with your kids? Is it a relax-with-a-movie kind of day, hanging out in the house in your pjs with nobody calling your name? Coming up with a perfect day sounds easy on the surface, but you may not have had a perfect day in years, or maybe ever. So, this may take some time and thought.

If a genie was in front of you and was willing to give

you a 24-hour period designed and executed just the way you say, what exactly would you ask for? Write it down as bullet points or brainstorm it as a picture—whatever way works for you. This one will change over time. As your relationship with your child gets better, or you learn more about yourself, you will think of new things you want to include in your perfect day.

Your People: An Exercise

The last list I want you to make is a list of the people in your life right now who are supportive and non-judgmental. They are the people who lift you up when you are around them and inspire you to be happier and healthier. Full disclosure here: this list will be really small. Like most of us, you've probably shut out many people. You've learned who you can talk to and who you can tell things to, and that's a handful of close friends or family members. So, don't worry if your list is small. Mine was too. Just know that, as with the other lists, this one will grow and change with time.

Now that you have started these lists, you're probably wondering what you are going to do with them. What is their purpose? Here it is—here is the answer: Now you know what you like, the things that are truly yours, and who you want to be around those who lift you up. Now you can start to bring more of these things and people into your life to free yourself from isolation.

When we talked about getting out and doing things

and inviting people in, it probably seemed like a scary thing to do or think about because you didn't know where to start. Now you do. Let's say you have identified that you like going for walks on your list. And you've identified someone who makes you feel happy to be around. Now you can very easily go for a walk when you need to get out. You can even ask that friend to join you. As you and your child adjust to this change, your available time increases, and you can be out of the house longer and longer.

Once I started my lists, I referred to them often. Walks with friends were on my like list. I increased my time and my distance from the house: starting with just going to the end of my street, to being out for a walk with a friend for an hour. Then I added going for coffee after my walk. I started to discover things about myself each day as I got out more and more. Before I knew it, I looked down at my like list and saw that I had made it all the way to 100 things that I *knew* I liked. They were my things!

This list of likes becomes so important. As you start changing your reactions to and your communication with your child, you will start to have more freedom away from your house. You will use these things to fill your cup, so to speak. They will make you feel stronger and allow you to enjoy your freedom. But best of all, you will be able to do things without your child without constantly worrying about what's going on at home. This will help you start to feel better about you and all the work you have done.

Imagine going from what feels like being a prisoner in your own home to having the freedom to go anywhere you want, for as long as you want, with or without your child. Doesn't that sound great?

Now don't get me wrong, this doesn't mean things are fixed or perfect. Something will come up. You will fall off the wagon, so to speak. Your child will be waiting for this and will pounce, eager to engage you in arguing and guilt. But that's fine. You will start to recognize how quickly you can bring yourself back to center, now that you are armed with the knowledge that it's possible you can.

Always keep in mind how far you have come when this happens. Your first reaction will be to be hard on yourself and to focus on what you consider to be a failure. You will tell yourself you failed; you can't do this; this isn't working. That thinking will be wrong. You can do this, and you have. Just give yourself 30 seconds to breathe and remind yourself how far you have come. Remember the freedom you have had and the changes you have seen. You know this is working. You know this is changing your life for the better. Don't get sucked back into the disappoint that comes with falling off the wagon.

You are human. You will not be perfect and on guard all day, every day. You will get comfortable with your new life, your new reality, and then you will forget that your child needs some extra care. It's ok to forget sometimes. Even I forget sometimes. The key here is how quickly you regain your strength and get back on track. That's what counts. At first this may take a couple days, but over time you will realize, right smack dab in the middle of an argument, that you are falling off the wagon, and you will catch yourself before you fall.

Your list of likes is exactly what you need to get started when you are coming out of isolation, and it is also what you will need when you fall off the wagon. Use this list when you need to get away. Use it when you need a break or need to think. This list is full of things you like and people you can call to build you back up. They are there to encourage you and show you how far you have come when you can't quite see it for yourself.

When you use this list, you will start to see that, after you come back from an activity or time away, you will be back on track. You will remember why you started this journey, and you will be back on track with your plan to have a happier and healthier relationship with yourself and your child.

Releasing Negativity

The other thing that happens at this stage is letting go of negative, unhealthy relationships that you were holding onto so that you could have someone to complain to who would sympathize. These relationships were never there in a healthy way. They were never there to help you find a healthy solution. They were, upon reflection, only there to allow you to wallow in your pain and self-pity. They supported your need to allow this behaviour from your child, and your continued "support" for your child. They allowed a place to complain in a way that was not taking action, but instead merely venting so that you could get the stuff you were dealing with off your chest.

Not all of the relationships you have will fall into that category, but be aware that as you start changing your relationship with your child for the better, those people who were supportive of it when things were at their worst will not necessarily be as supportive about things getting better. You may find that this becomes the group that is most judgmental about the changes you have made and are making. They will start to repeat to you all things that you have been through and all the reasons you had for staying in it for long, just the way it was.

Your relationship with your child can and will be a healthy one with respected boundaries and without excuses, resentment, and tiptoeing around your child's moods. But it will be different than the one you had before mental illness arose. It might sound nice if things could go back to the time before all this started, but in truth, this new relationship will be so much better. It will be stronger and definitely healthier! Remember, it is going to take work and consistency, but you are strong and you can get there.

An Exercise

Let's go back to your lists as a closing exercise for this chapter. Take one of the likes from your list and go do it.

Spend some time with yourself or a friend. Get out of the house and enjoy yourself with something you enjoy from your list.

Bonus optional exercise: Ask your child to do make a similar list. Ask them to write down a list of things they enjoy. You may find later, if they let you see it, that you have some things in common. That creates a perfect opportunity to get out with your child and find some common ground. But this one is up to you. If you think your child is ready, try it. Honestly, the worst that might happen is they will say no. And that is ok too.

CHAPTER 11

Your Other Child

Even though I grew up learning to be afraid of mental illness taking someone I loved, it took me a long time to realize mental illness had moved into my house. At first, I wasn't sure what was happening. I was just trying to figure out what was going on with Codi, which then became an ongoing "need" to help Codi and "fix" things for Codi. In writing this book, I saw the last seven to nine years of my life more clearly in a way I couldn't before. There were a lot of things that I was still unsure about and hadn't dealt with or even acknowledged. This was solely based on me being so consumed by what was happening with Codi that nothing else around me seemed to matter anymore.

It became painfully apparent to me while writing this book that I had completely neglected my oldest son.

As mentioned, I have two children, both boys, and Codi with Codi's mental illness or figuring out what was even going on, before I knew enough to call it a mental illness, I completely forgot about Zachary. I knew he was there, of course, and what was going on with him, but he didn't have the same mom that Codi had.

If you were to sit my boys down and ask them what their mom was like, I'm not sure they would describe the same person. I mean, sure, they would give you similar qualities or traits, but Zachary really missed out growing up. Zachary almost became another support person instead of Codi's brother or my son.

Looking back, I can see that I felt like I lost my son to mental illness. But for Zachary, he lost his mom to mental illness in a different way.

During the course of writing this book, it hit me like a ton of bricks, that I wasn't as good of a mom to Zachary as I was to Codi, in my eyes at least. So, I made sure to reach out and let Zachary know that I now can acknowledge it and that I'm sorry for not being there.

I did the regular stuff like baths and dinners, brushing teeth, and supporting my sons in baseball or whatever sport they wanted. I made it to most of the games and was the crazy parent making all the noise cheering on my child or yelling at the referee when I didn't like a call. I was there for both of my boys when they called for anything or were sick. That part of who their mother is, they would both describe the same. The mom who was different is harder to define and explain.

It was like triage: I paid more attention to the son who seemed to need it most. Everything and everyone else seemed to be secondary to that. Codi needed the attention, the appointments, the constant care, and worrying about.

Even though I don't know that I would or could have done differently, I can still look back and see that Zachary didn't get the same things or the same care that Codi got. Zachry was constantly told to let things go, to not be angry at his brother, to be more understanding of what his brother was going through. Zachary wasn't allowed the same leeway that Codi was. Zachary was always told that he was the oldest and had to set an example, or that he had to wait for my attention because I had something to do with Codi.

As I wrote this book and came to this realization, I made sure to let Zachary know that he is also my whole world. I told him exactly how important to me he is, and that I am truly sorry for all the sacrifices he made over the years. In all the raw emotion that come out while writing this book, what changed for Zachary was definitely the hardest to deal with.

You might remember that both my sons ran away. Codi came back by police escort, but Zachary decided to make the change permanent. He moved in, first with his dad and then my aunt, so he could return to high school in Hamilton with the rest of his friends from growing up. Once Zachary moved out of my aunt's house, he started living on his own. I have helped him and been there for him when he needed something, but that doesn't change that Zachary didn't have it the way Codi did.

Who Have You Set Aside?

I'm sure you may be thinking of the people in your life who fit a similar story. Maybe your family or spouse, friends or co-workers. If you think about it long enough, you can probably think of someone or a group of people whom you've put aside to make sure that your child with mental illness is getting everything you can possibly think of.

It isn't too late for me to be Zachary's mom, but he is 18 now and out on his own. He just needs a different mom now than he did when he was 10. Don't get me wrong. I have a great relationship with both of my boys today. They are both amazing people. I am so very proud of them for the things they have each accomplished.

As important as it is for me to talk about all the ways I recovered *with* Codi and all the strategies I used to get here, it is equally important for me to share that when you have two or more children, and each of those children don't have mental health issues, the "healthy" ones lose out too. There may be other relationships that you have pushed aside to take care of your child with mental illness as well. You are going to want to start reaching out to these people and repairing these relationships. Many will tell you that they did and do understand. But the fact is, mental illness affects them too. It's important to acknowledge that.

As parents, we do what we believe is necessary, and we do it almost without thinking about it. Our gut instinct takes over, and we go into robot mom mode. We do what we think and feel is best for the child who struggles. We don't even recognize or notice the child who gets shoved to the side and even slightly forgotten about. We just assume that they will understand and see that their brother or sister needs us more.

Reach Out

Realize that if you've done this, you have the ability to change this behaviour. Start with a conversation with that "forgotten" child. You must show them that you realize, acknowledge, and apologize for your behaviour. When I did this, I was overwhelmed with both a deep sadness and a great pride. I sent Zachary a text, just before I realized I needed to add this chapter, apologizing for not being a good mom. I apologized for not being there for him when I should have been, when he needed me. Zachary responded back with the best possible text. It was more than I could have imagined or even hoped for. He told me that he understood why I wasn't there, and said he knew that I felt I needed to be there more for Codi. He said he has become who he is because of what he had and didn't have growing up and is glad he is who he is. He then made sure I knew that when it counted for him, I was always there.

You see, if you never talk to them, if you never tell them you are sorry, you will always live in fear of the reaction you are afraid you might get. You will live in the guilt and shame of having sacrificed one child's need for the other's. You will project what you think and feel on your children or on your family because you will never know how understanding they can be. Having that conversation with Zachary taught me a couple important lessons. First, it taught me that I have raised *two* amazing boys who are filled with such love and compassion for people. Second, it taught me that I can have different relationships with my children, and it is ok. They don't have to be the same, they don't have to have the same things, and they don't have to have the same mom in order for them to come out of the struggle with mental illness.

Finally, I learned that mental illness did not win! I won. I have a beautiful family, and they are loving and supportive and will always be together. I know this because, if ever there was something that was tough enough to break us down and rip us apart, it was the struggle of mental illness. Mental illness can only win if you give up, if you let it, and if you give it the power to do so.

Taking Back Your Power

I took back the power. I chose to make sure that I came out on top of the struggle with mental illness. The full and complete message here is to learn and to believe that every day you will learn something new. Another layer of learning and raw emotion will happen along the way. When it does, embrace it, learn from it, and release it so you can continue to live, grow, and be happy with your new relationship with your child who struggles with mental illness *and* your other child(ren).

An Exercise

I have one final task for you to complete here. This task is going to be reaching out to your other child. You may not be ready for a full-on conversation yet, but reach out and make some time to be with just your other child. Plan some time for just the two of you. Or you could write a letter to your other child. Tell them everything you are ready to say. Trust me when I tell you that no matter which of the two you pick, you will be so thankful you did this. And then expand on it. Like dating, before you end your time with your child, ask when you will be able to do this with just them again. Make a plan with them, and stick to it. You will enjoy every minute of it! I know from experience how much this fills my heart with love and joy. Now my time with Zachary is exactly that: my time with just Zachary!

Conclusion

When I started this journey, I felt hopeless, like nothing and no one could help me or understand me. I felt like no one could change this life for me or make it better. I thought the chaos was forever my reality, the life I would have from now on—or at least until my son could "grow out of it." I doubted that it would ever get any better and feared that at some point I was going to lose my son to mental illness, or worse, suicide. Through the process I've outlined for you, I came to the realization that I could fix only me, and that was good enough. The realization, that I didn't make my son this way, was exactly what I needed.

As parents, we want to believe that we can fix everything that happens to our child(ren). When we can't fix it, it must be because we did something wrong. We must be bad parents. We look back at all the decisions we've made, and we wonder whether, if we'd done something different, our child wouldn't be like this.

I hope you understand by now that none of that is true. None of that exists outside of your head. You are, as we all are, the hardest on yourself. You must realize that you did the best you could, that each decision you made was with the knowledge you had at the time, and that it was the best decision you could have made then. Every second that passes provides you with new information, and that information can change a decision. But you cannot change the past. You can only use the present information to change the way you react to the present.

I look back now and see all of the things that I had to let go of in order to have the life I have now, to have the relationship I have with my son. I have no regrets about what I have been through to get where my boys and I are today. I now see that I wouldn't have been able to continue as I was and have a healthy relationship with my son.

I lost friends because I was told I wasn't being a good friend to them. I had to leave the relationship I was in because I realized I really didn't want it or the life it provided. I realized that some of the people in my life didn't provide the right set of boundaries I wanted my son to see, and they didn't provide the right influence for me or my children.

I have tried and tested these strategies and others. These are the ones that I found worked, for me and each of my clients, every time. These strategies helped me get to where I am today. I am able to share space with my son. We are able to talk and laugh together. And he tells me every day that he loves me and thanks me for everything I have done for him. Both of my boys do.

This can be your outcome as well. It all starts with the willingness to change and to trust that, if you follow this plan, things will start to get better for you too. You are ready for this change. You want nothing more than for your child to get better, to be happy, and it all starts with you accepting that you are strong and you are able to change this. It starts with you. It starts with one step forward. As you implement each step, it gets easier and easier.

Once you realize that you are the one who knows your child best, you can move forward without knowing exactly what diagnosis is in your future, if any. You are the one who sees the changes and notices the different behaviours before anyone. You are the one who is going to all the different appointments and filling in everyone involved on everything that happens, as it is happening. You have searched for answers for so long and wondered for so long when those answers will come, but you have the tools to start changing the dynamic of your house and your relationship with your child right now.

You now understand that your child isn't "bad." They are just behaving badly, and, just like with any behaviour, there is hope for change. There is a way to help your child see the way to change their behaviour for the better. As you start to separate your child from their behaviour and their emotions, things will start to change and get better and easier. Not only will you start to see when your child changing, but you will start to accept that changes are possible. Your child will start to think more and more about their behaviours because they are no longer able to blame you. They will start to understand that they are responsible for what they do.

When we recognize that even as adults we gave a hard time controlling our emotions, we start to have an understanding about the kind of struggle our child is going through. By recognizing this and separating them from their actions and behaviours, we hold them accountable for their choices.

Then come the changes that occur when you start to change your reactions to and your communications with your child. By allowing them time to think things through; by allowing them to be responsible for their own actions, you will give them the opportunity to think before acting, instead of after. This brings about change. When they see that you are no longer willing to listen to them explain their crazy way of thinking and behaving, they will stop telling you about it. When there is no one to listen, there is no reason to behave like that anymore. Slowly, your child's behaviour starts to change, and your reactions become more intentional. The way you talk to your child changes. All of a sudden, you look around and are just in a better space. You can now see that the way you react and communicate with your child is vital for a healthier relationship. It is the way to being healthy for both of you.

Being in a better place allows you to talk about what is happening in your life in a healthy way. It allows you to be able to step outside the chaos. You are no longer ashamed about what you are going through. You are able to tell people what things are like for you. Talking about what life was like for you doesn't seem so bad anymore because it isn't where you are now. You learn to stop hiding and start allowing people to come into your home. You start making and following through with plans.

You see that your life and your story have an impact on your household and your relationship with your child. You see how everything that has unfolded has set you up to be in this space with your child. That then becomes the blueprint for what you need to do to fix things. By creating boundaries and changing any self-defeating behaviours you have developed along the way, you are able to create a better you and a better relationship with your child and with all those around you. You will hold your relationships to a higher standard.

You can look at the lists you made, the list of 50 things, the perfect day, and the list of people in your life who are truly supportive in a positive way and know without a doubt that these things will allow you to discover who you are. You will learn how to be fully yourself, not just a mother who has a child with issues. You will no longer be defined by your child's mental illness, and neither will your child. When you discover things about yourself, like things you like to do, and you are real about who in your life is there to support you rather than let you settle for the way you have been living, you will be able to step out of the isolation. You will get out more, do more, be more happy more often, and be able to step away when things are not going so well. You will start to find yourself, and by discovering who you are, your relationship with your child will just get better, and the changes will become easier and easier to make.

I hope that you are now able to see that by looking at your behaviours and your story and actively working on changing yourself, that you will be able to show your child the way to a happier and healthier life. By putting boundaries in place, caring for yourself, and doing things that make you feel good, you are setting a great example for your child. Your child is watching you right now, whether you think so or not. They are still learning from you, and they will start to implement the changes in their lives they see you implement in yours.

Things aren't going to change overnight. Be patient—you have to start somewhere. Before you know it, you will look around and see that life is better than you have believed it could be for quite some time. Change starts with one decision, one action, one step in the right direction. Change starts with you and it takes time. Continue moving forward, even when you think its not working and you feel like giving up. One step at a time. Focus on one step, and when you get the hang of that, move on to the next step. Always remember any step is a step in the right direction because it means moving, and right now you are hiding. Hiding is not moving.

We have touched on everything in this book and how it has and will benefit you. By now you may have already started to implement some of these changes, or maybe you read this straight through because you are anxious to know how it all plays out for you and your child. Either way, I hope you are feeling a sense of renewed hope for your life and your relationship with your child.

I have tried many different strategies, most have not worked, but these are the ones that I found worked best and were most effective for me with my son. These are the ones I use in my program to help my clients who are struggling just like you are now and just like I was.

You may be thinking all of this sounds great, but that you want to have someone who can help you through this. For me, my coach made all the difference in the world. If you have someone in your life who can help you through this and be there for you when you need the extra support, then I encourage you to reach out to them. If not, and you want to find a coach, please reach out to me, and let's do this together.

If someone had asked me, even a year ago, if I would be where I am today with my son, I would have thought they were crazy. In fact, Codi and I often talk about where we were and the things we went through and the changes that we've both made over this last year. We are both so impressed with how far we have come—how far he has come. We have both done so well and come through so much that, when we look back, it seems like a totally different time.

Don't get me wrong, life isn't perfect for us yet, but we are definitely in a way better space then either of us could have imagined a year ago. I have implemented all of these changes, and over the course of this last year, I have taken steps has changed my relationship with my son as well as changed who I am as a person and a mother. I have always been strong, but now I know I can survive anything. And my son knows that we will always get through anything, together.

I am no longer afraid to get out of bed and am able to walk by Codi's room without wondering if this is the time I am going to find my son dead. I know that we have found a way to live peacefully together, for the most part, without a clear diagnosis. We are able to talk and laugh and tell each other what we mean to each other without his eyes rolling in disgust. I am no longer afraid of my child, and I am no longer afraid *for* my child. I have found my son again!

Acknowledgments

This book has brought me a greater appreciation for the strength and understanding I have met with in my life and for those to whom I am grateful to be sharing the journey. I am so grateful to God, who has given me this amazing life as well as those in it. I have been given this amazing gift of being able to help other mothers who are just like I was, struggling to find the light in the darkness of mental illness, and for that I will always be thankful. I am so grateful to be able to share my journey and the discoveries I have made that have helped me and my son.

I would like to thank my boys, Zachary and Codi. I am extremely lucky to have you both and am so proud of who you have become. I can't thank you enough for allowing me to share our journey to help others. I couldn't have asked for anything more than the love and support I have received from each of you. You have both taught me so much about myself and about love and have made me so proud to be your mother. You are both such amazing and caring people. The way that you have each grown overflows my heart with love you both. You are both so wise, far beyond your years. I love you both with all my heart.

I would also like to thank my parents: my dad, John, and my mom and stepdad, John and Catherine. I would not be who I am today without the love, support, and guidance from the three of you. I could not have made it through all of this without each and every one of you. I am so blessed to be able to say you are my parents. Thank you for all of your advice and wisdom and for being there for me whenever I needed you no matter what that meant, and even when I didn't know I needed it. You have all been a great inspiration for me. Also, I am so grateful for my siblings, John, Jessica, and David. The love and support from you have been unconditional. I am so lucky to have you all in my life and to be able to say that you are all, not only my family, but also my friends. You have shown my boys and me the value of having great family and great support. You have always been there no matter what and have shown my boys that love is judgment-free, always. I couldn't have asked for better role models for my children.

To the rest of my family, I want to say thank you for all you have done for me. God gave me such a great, loving family, and I am so grateful for you all. To my aunt and uncle who shared my deep profound conversation and helped me out of my fear: I am eternally grateful for you both, more than words could ever express.

An immense amount of gratitude goes to my amazing coach, mentor, and friend, Tamara. You have shown me a life I never even knew was possible. You have helped me see that I was stronger than I thought, and you stood by me while I rediscovered myself and a healthier relationship with my son. Thank you for believing in me and never letting me give up on myself. Thank you for giving me the confidence to share my voice with the world. You have shown me how big my dreams can be. You are a true gift from God.

Thank you to all my girls—you know who you all are. We were brought together as soul sisters, all rediscovering ourselves and our paths. Along the way, we found each other, and the most amazing bonds were formed. We haven't needed to know each other for a lifetime, but I feel like you all have given me a lifetime's worth of love and support. Thank you all for sharing in my journey. You are all the most beautiful souls.

To my beautiful editor, Maggie: You have been so amazing to me and made this process so fun, even through the difficult times and tears. I couldn't have done this without you and your guidance. You have shown me the true power of sharing and have shown me the value of my voice. You have shown me the strength and wisdom I have to share and have inspired me to be the best writer I can be. Thank you for making this a dream come true.

Finally, thank you to everyone in my life, past or present, who has helped and shared this journey with me. I know we were brought together for a reason, and I am eternally grateful for all of you. You all have a part in who

I am today. The laughter, tears, and lessons we taught each other have helped me to be the best me I can be.

About the Author

Corrie Corrigan was born and raised in Hamilton, Ontario, and moved to St. Catharines, Ontario, in 2014, where she fell in love with the city. A first-time author, she is the founder of Clear Choice Coaching & Wellness, where she helps moms of children with mental illness release what's in the way, recover their identities, and create healthy relationships with their kids. She also works with Multi-Level Marketers (MLM) to help them create thriving businesses, so they can make more money and spend more time with their families. Corrie has a passion for energy healing work and has been a reiki practitioner since 2017. She has two teenage sons, and loves nature, country music, and dancing.

Thank You

I'm so grateful you took the time to read this book. It outlines a program I've developed as a result of my journey. The program features the strategies I've written about here, as well as others. It is designed to guide you and support you through your "recovery" from mental illness. Working together, we can get clear on where you are now and find a path forward that doesn't overwhelm you. You'll build a better relationship with your child and a better one with yourself.

As a thank you to you, I'd like to offer you a complimentary discovery call—a conversation in which we can talk about *you* and assess the next move that feels good to you.

To get your Free Strategy Session, contact me here:

- clearchoicecoachingwellness@gmail.com
- https://www.facebook.com/corrie.corrigan
- https://clearchoicecoachingwellness.ca